T0129599

An Analysis of

CK Prahalad
& Gary Hamel's

The Core Competence
of the Corporation

The Macat Team

Published by Macat International Ltd
24:13 Coda Centre, 189 Munster Road, London SW6 6AW.

Distributed exclusively by Routledge
2 Park Square, Milton Park, Abingdon, Oxon OX14 4RN
711 Third Avenue, New York, NY 10017, USA

Routledge is an imprint of the Taylor & Francis Group, an informa business

www.macat.com
info@macat.com

Cataloguing in Publication Data
A catalogue record for this book is available from the British Library.
Library of Congress Cataloguing-in-Publication Data is available upon request.
Cover illustration: Etienne Gilfillan

ISBN 978-1-912302-19-2 (hardback)
ISBN 978-1-912127-12-2 (paperback)
ISBN 978-1-912281-07-7 (e-book)

Notice
The information in this book is designed to orientate readers of the work under analysis,
to elucidate and contextualise its key ideas and themes, and to aid in the development
of critical thinking skills. It is not meant to be used, nor should it be used, as a
substitute for original thinking or in place of original writing or research. References and
notes are provided for informational purposes and their presence does not constitute
endorsement of the information or opinions therein. This book is presented solely for
educational purposes. It is sold on the understanding that the publisher is not engaged
to provide any scholarly advice. The publisher has made every effort to ensure that
this book is accurate and up-to-date, but makes no warranties or representations with
regard to the completeness or reliability of the information it contains. The information
and the opinions provided herein are not guaranteed or warranted to produce particular
results and may not be suitable for students of every ability. The publisher shall not be
liable for any loss, damage or disruption arising from any errors or omissions, or from
the use of this book, including, but not limited to, special, incidental, consequential or
other damages caused, or alleged to have been caused, directly or indirectly, by the
information contained within.

CONTENTS

THE MACAT LIBRARY

The Macat Library is a series of unique academic explorations of seminal works in the humanities and social sciences – books and papers that have had a significant and widely recognised impact on their disciplines. It has been created to serve as much more than just a summary of what lies between the covers of a great book. It illuminates and explores the influences on, ideas of, and impact of that book. Our goal is to offer a learning resource that encourages critical thinking and fosters a better, deeper understanding of important ideas.

Each publication is divided into three Sections: Influences, Ideas, and Impact. Each Section has four Modules. These explore every important facet of the work, and the responses to it.

This Section-Module structure makes a Macat Library book easy to use, but it has another important feature. Because each Macat book is written to the same format, it is possible (and encouraged!) to cross-reference multiple Macat books along the same lines of inquiry or research. This allows the reader to open up interesting interdisciplinary pathways.

To further aid your reading, lists of glossary terms and people mentioned are included at the end of this book (these are indicated by an asterisk [*] throughout) – as well as a list of works cited.

Macat has worked with the University of Cambridge to identify the elements of critical thinking and understand the ways in which six different skills combine to enable effective thinking.
Three allow us to fully understand a problem; three more give us the tools to solve it. Together, these six skills make up the **PACIER** model of critical thinking. They are:

ANALYSIS – understanding how an argument is built
EVALUATION – exploring the strengths and weaknesses of an argument
INTERPRETATION – understanding issues of meaning

CREATIVE THINKING – coming up with new ideas and fresh connections
PROBLEM-SOLVING – producing strong solutions
REASONING – creating strong arguments

To find out more, visit **WWW.MACAT.COM.**

CRITICAL THINKING AND
THE CORE COMPETENCE OF THE CORPORATION

Primary critical thinking skill: EVALUATION
Secondary critical thinking skill: REASONING

C.K. Prahalad and Gary Hamel's 1990 "The Core Competence of the Corporation" helped redefine traditional ideas of management strategy. It did so by focusing companies on one of the key critical thinking skills: evaluation. In critical thinking, evaluation is all about judging the strengths and weaknesses of arguments – assessing their reasoning and the relevance or adequateness of the evidence they use. For Prahalad and Hamel, companies could gain a competitive edge by evaluating themselves: their own strengths and weaknesses. By sensitively evaluating core competencies – the collective knowledge inside the organization that distinguishes it from other corporations – they could target efforts and resources with strategic focus.

For Prahalad and Hamel, managers need to be able to identify and evaluate their company's unique skill sets, and the technologies that distinguish them from others businesses. How well they then coordinate these elements defines a company's competitive strength and how quickly it can adapt to new challenges. As Prahalad and Hamel showed in their case studies, the critical thinking skill of evaluation – knowing what you do best, how well you do it, and how you might improve – is absolutely central to staying ahead of the crowd.

ABOUT THE AUTHORS OF THE ORIGINAL WORK

C. K. Prahalad was born in 1941 in India and was educated first in the country of his birth, and then in the United States. **Gary Hamel** was born in the US in 1954 and was taught by Prahalad at the University of Michigan's Ross School of Business. The two men struck up a friendship and co-authored a number of influential business strategy books and articles. Prahalad died in 2010, but Hamel remains an important business figure. Forbes magazine has nominated him as one of "The 10 Most Influential Business Gurus."

ABOUT MACAT

GREAT WORKS FOR CRITICAL THINKING

Macat is focused on making the ideas of the world's great thinkers accessible and comprehensible to everybody, everywhere, in ways that promote the development of enhanced critical thinking skills.

It works with leading academics from the world's top universities to produce new analyses that focus on the ideas and the impact of the most influential works ever written across a wide variety of academic disciplines. Each of the works that sit at the heart of its growing library is an enduring example of great thinking. But by setting them in context – and looking at the influences that shaped their authors, as well as the responses they provoked – Macat encourages readers to look at these classics and game-changers with fresh eyes. Readers learn to think, engage and challenge their ideas, rather than simply accepting them.

'Macat offers an amazing first-of-its-kind tool for interdisciplinary learning and research. Its focus on works that transformed their disciplines and its rigorous approach, drawing on the world's leading experts and educational institutions, opens up a world-class education to anyone.'

Andreas Schleicher
Director for Education and Skills, Organisation for Economic
Co-operation and Development

'Macat is taking on some of the major challenges in university education … They have drawn together a strong team of active academics who are producing teaching materials that are novel in the breadth of their approach.'

Prof Lord Broers,
former Vice-Chancellor of the University of Cambridge

'The Macat vision is exceptionally exciting. It focuses upon new modes of learning which analyse and explain seminal texts which have profoundly influenced world thinking and so social and economic development. It promotes the kind of critical thinking which is essential for any society and economy. This is the learning of the future.'

Rt Hon Charles Clarke, former UK Secretary of State for Education

'The Macat analyses provide immediate access to the critical conversation surrounding the books that have shaped their respective discipline, which will make them an invaluable resource to all of those, students and teachers, working in the field.'

Professor William Tronzo, University of California at San Diego

WAYS IN TO THE TEXT

KEY POINTS

- C. K. Prahalad and Gary Hamel combined academic careers with the establishment of successful consulting firms in the fields of innovation and strategy* (methods of planning business affairs with the aim of achieving specific goals such as profit, growth, or market dominance).

- Published in 1990, the article "The Core Competence of the Corporation" uses empirical evidence (that is, evidence verified by observation) gathered by the authors to provide a compelling argument for how corporations can gain a competitive advantage* in the marketplace.

- "The Core Competence of the Corporation" is one of the most reprinted articles in the history of the *Harvard Business Review** and paved the way for advances in the study of strategic management.*

Who Are C. K. Prahalad and Gary Hamel?

"The Core Competence of the Corporation" (1990) is an article co-authored by the business scholars Coimbatore Krishnarao Prahalad and Gary Hamel. The two collaborated on many books and articles dealing with business strategy.*

Coimbatore Krishnarao Prahalad (1941–2010) was born in India. He was educated first in his country of birth and then in the United

States. Although he wanted to pursue a career in India, political unrest there during the 1970s spurred him to return to the United States in 1977. As Harvey C. Fruehauf Professor of Business Administration at the University of Michigan, he was honored with a Lifetime Achievement Award by the Ross School of Business and received numerous honorary doctorates and honors, including the Padma Bhushan,* one of India's highest civilian awards.

He worked as consultant for many of the world's leading companies and served on the board of directors of the American technology company NCR, the consumer goods company Hindustan Unilever, and the World Resources Institute,* a non-governmental research organization founded to promote prosperity through the management of sustainable natural resources.

Gary Hamel was born in 1954 and educated in the United States. He joined the London Business School in 1983 and remains on the faculty to this day, teaching global strategy*—the theoretical and practical means of conducting business across international markets with the aim of meeting aims and obligations specific to the business in question.

Hamel obtained his doctoral degree at the Ross School of Business, University of Michigan, where he studied under Prahalad. Both men shared an interest in strategic management (the means by which business is deliberately conducted with the aim of achieving specific goals and targets) and wanted to understand why some companies were more successful than others. This shared interest led to the two men co-authoring 12 books and journal articles.

Hamel pursued a career as a business consultant in tandem with his academic and writing career, working with major international corporations. In 1994 he founded Strateos, a consulting firm working in the field of innovation and strategy. More recently Hamel started the Management Innovation eXchange, an organization that aims to "reinvent" management for the twenty-first century.

What Does "The Core Competence of the Corporation" Say?

"The Core Competence of the Corporation" aims to show business managers how to be successful in a competitive environment. It offers a practical argument for identifying what are called a corporation's "core competencies"*—the collective knowledge inside the organization that distinguishes it from other corporations and that can be used to produce a competitive advantage. A "competitive advantage" is simply an advantage that an organization has over its competitors, allowing it to achieve greater sales, for example, or to retain more customers, than its competition.

This collective knowledge, or "learning," that defines a corporation's core competencies, can be thought of as knowledge of *skills* and *technologies*. How well or otherwise managers coordinate these elements defines a company's competitive advantage. The authors argue that if a corporation focuses on its competencies, then it can adapt much more quickly to new situations. Core competencies are the basis for the development of competitive products—but what makes a product competitive? Products must be unique, they must be distinguishable from their competitors' products, and they must provide value to customers.

The core competence of the Japanese company Honda lies in engines, for example. This gives it a distinct advantage in businesses involving engines (this might be companies connected with motorcycles, lawn mowers, or generators, say). The Japanese company Canon has core competencies in optics, imaging, and microprocessor controls, which have enabled it to enter related markets such as copiers, laser printers, cameras, and image scanners. In some cases, Canon has come to dominate these markets.

Core competencies span business portfolios* within a corporation as well as its products, and can support several businesses and/or products; they are more stable and evolve much more slowly than products, which are at the heart of a corporation's core competencies;

and they are gained and developed by continual work—they are the collective learning of the corporation, and are enhanced by working together. We can consider market competition concerning products to be just the surface expression of a fierce fight over competencies.

In the text, Prahalad and Hamel also introduce the idea of a "strategic architecture,"* which they describe as a "road map" to the future. Strategic architecture both identifies which competencies ought to be developed to gain key competitive advantages and determines the technology, staffing, and other resources required to support these competencies.

Strategic architecture provides the framework for achieving a competitive advantage. The term embodies both "leadership" and "corporate culture"* (the vision and principles that members of an organization subscribe to that help define their collective identity). Both of these things are essential to a successful corporation.

Prahalad and Hamel illustrate the need for *all* company resources to be available to any part or division of the same company. Only then can competencies be exploited with any effect. The traditional structure of the large, conglomerate businesses to which the book is directed comprises business "portfolios"—self-contained administrative offices, departments, and offshoot businesses. But in this structure only money is shared and precious little else.

"The Core Competence" proposes "rethinking the corporation," which requires both looking at the outward structure of a corporation and identifying and building competencies—core strengths. It concludes by looking at the inward structure or management of the corporation, which requires knowledge of how to exploit competencies in order to build competitive advantage.

Why Does "The Core Competence of the Corporation" Matter?

The concept of a "core competence" has become a common term used in most management theories. Examples are "human resource management"* (the management of the people who work for a business with the aim of most effectively achieving a business's goals) and "knowledge management"* (the means by which organizational knowledge is obtained, pooled, developed, and employed in order to achieve specific business goals).

"The Core Competence," with its practical analysis of strategy and leadership, is a "how-to" on gaining and maintaining a competitive advantage. It explains how Apple out-strategized its rival American technology and computer company IBM and why companies such as Sony, Honda, and Canon have been so successful.

The Internet search engine Google did not exist at the time Prahalad and Hamel wrote this article. Yet it owes much of its success to following the ideas first contained in "The Core Competence." Despite pursuing several seemingly unrelated projects, from self-driving vehicles to Google Glass, Google has focused on maintaining and evolving its core competencies over time and has utilized its corporate culture and internal talent to drive innovation in many areas.

The paper has had an impact at an academic level, leading to the development of new schools of thought within the field of strategic management, notably the "capability-based"* school (which focuses on core competencies), the "resource-based"* approach (which focuses on internal resources), and "new games" strategies* (a school of thought that maintains that competitive advantage is generated internally, through constant innovation in both products and services and working processes).

In "The Core Competence," Prahalad and Hamel also expanded the scope of what might be considered "strategy." "Knowledge management," "corporate culture," and "organizational learning"*— the process by which knowledge is developed and shared in an organization—can perhaps be considered subdivisions of strategy that owe something to the article's analysis and arguments.

The article offers the essential message that corporations are not defined by what they *do*, but by what they *know*. This is as relevant today as it was in 1990 when the paper first appeared. It will continue to be relevant, because it is a question of nurturing skills that create value within a company's own walls and establishing qualities unique to it.

Two major business areas have developed out of the idea of creating core competencies.

Identifying core competencies logically and inevitably results in identifying *non*-core competencies. This has led to outsourcing* (that is, contracting out these non-core competencies to third parties) with the creation of an entire support industry as a result. Corporations must focus on developing and maintaining core competencies to remain competitive in the long term.

In order to achieve this, they must also aim to improve their processes and practices. The general adoption of this principle has led to a sub-industry of continuous improvement, re-engineering* (that is, adjustments to the business's workflow for the sake of things such as cost and efficiency in production and decision-making), and lean management (an approach that seeks to refine an organization's basic systems to maximize customer value while minimizing waste).

Since "The Core Competence" was first published in 1990, the notions of "outsourcing," "re-engineering," and "transformation"* (the process of altering a business in fundamental ways to address changes in the market) have become standard management terms and strategies. It is not possible to state definitively what future management strategies will be, but it will likely be that they will rely on two ideas: first, on knowledge accumulated in an organization (core competence) and, second, on a plan to reach the stated goal (strategic architecture).

SECTION 1
INFLUENCES

MODULE 1
THE AUTHORS AND
THE HISTORICAL CONTEXT

KEY POINTS

- The article "The Core Competence of the Corporation" redefined the concept of management strategy by focusing less on traditional business theory and more on how to make use of a company's collective knowledge.

- C. K. Prahalad and Gary Hamel shared an interest in "strategic management."* They were fascinated by what it was in leadership that made some corporations excel and others fall behind.

- A driving idea behind the article was this: was the success of Japanese companies over Western companies a mystery, or could it be easily explained?

Why Read This Text?

Published in 1990, the business scholars C. K. Prahalad and Gary Hamel's article "The Core Competence of the Corporation" transformed corporate strategy. As relevant today as when it was first published, it is one of the most reprinted articles ever to be published by respected management magazine *Harvard Business Review*.*[1]

In their article, Prahalad and Hamel urge corporate executives to "identify, cultivate, and exploit the core competencies* that make growth possible."[2] Building on their groundbreaking 1989 article "Strategic Intent," ideas proposed in "The Core Competence" were further developed in their subsequent book, *Competing for the Future* (1994). This publication famously showcased how the American computer company IBM found itself completely blindsided by Apple,

> **❝ If you read nothing else, read [this article] from HBR's most influential authors … "The Core Competence of the Corporation", by C. K. Prahalad and Gary Hamel. ❞**
>
> *Harvard Business Review, HBR's 10 Must Reads: The Essentials*

now a technology giant, because it failed to see the potential of the personal computer after becoming absorbed by the idea of maintaining an apparently unassailable leadership in the business of building and selling mainframes (high-performance computers used for large-scale computing purposes).

"The Core Competence" was the fifth of twelve texts co-authored by Prahalad and Hamel between 1983 and 1996. In it, they presented a brand new overview of competitiveness, the organization, and strategy* (planning business affairs with the aim of achieving specific goals such as profit, growth, or market dominance). While their peers were busy researching strategy from the strict basis of traditional economic theory, in which price and quality are paramount, they instead took a holistic approach, considering the organization's constituent parts—and specifically addressing the role and value of a corporation's collective knowledge. This collective knowledge (or "learning")—which, they argue, gives a corporation a competitive advantage* over other corporations in the marketplace—they term "core competence."

Both authors have combined their theoretical academic knowledge and real-world business experience to produce a seminal text.

Authors' Lives

Born on August 8, 1941 in the southern Indian state of Tamil Nadu, Coimbatore Krishnarao Prahalad (known as "C. K." throughout his life) was one of nine children. His father was a judge and prominent labor rights lawyer. A high achiever, Prahalad graduated from school three years ahead of schedule. By age 19—and equipped with a physics degree from Loyola College (part of the University of Madras in the Indian state of Chennai)—he joined the chemicals company Union Carbide (now a subsidiary of the Dow Chemical Company), where he worked for four years. As a manager on the assembly line, Prahalad created new production procedures that became the company's global gold standard.

With a PhD from Harvard Business School, in 1975 Prahalad went back to his native India. Initially intending to settle there with his wife and two children, Prahalad began to find the inward-looking and nationalist India of the 1970s somewhat oppressive. An internationalist by nature, he returned to the United States in 1977 and there developed a career in both academia and business. He was ranked by Thinkers50 as the world's "most influential business thinker" twice, in 2007 and 2009. He also served on numerous boards of directors as a consultant to large corporate businesses such as AT&T, Citicorp, Unilever, and Oracle, before his death of a lung-related disease in 2010. He was 68.

Born in 1954 in the United States, Gary Hamel was a hospital administrator before becoming an academic. He has a bachelor of science degree from Andrews University in Michigan and a master's degree in business administration from the University of Michigan, Hamel joined the staff of the London Business School in 1983 and taught global strategy* before graduating in 1990 with a PhD at the Ross School of Business, University of Michigan, where he studied under C. K. Prahalad. Both men soon found they shared an interest in strategic management and in understanding exactly *why* some corporations are more successful than others.

Hamel founded the strategy and innovation consulting firm Strategos in 1994. He has worked with global companies including

General Electric, Time Warner, Nestlé, Shell, Best Buy, Procter & Gamble, 3M, IBM, and Microsoft as a consultant and in management training, and is a frequent speaker at conferences, a regular voice in the media, and a government adviser on innovation and industrial competitiveness. Hamel is a *Harvard Business Review* star writer, being the most reprinted author in its history.[3]

Authors' Backgrounds

"The Core Competence of the Corporation" addressed a pressing issue of the time in which it was conceived: why were some Japanese businesses more successful than their counterparts in the United States? It clearly was not just an issue of what products they were making, but how a business was actually run.

After World War II* ended in 1945, the United States effectively ran Japan until 1952.[4] During this six-year period, the Western administration made three key changes that laid the foundations for Japan's rapid economic growth during the 1960s and 1970s: they abolished the *zaibatsu**—the Japanese industrial and financial business conglomerates that had previously monopolized industry; they implemented key land reforms; and they introduced new labor laws.

Ironically, American authorities *encouraged* business practices and industrial policies that later became a bone of contention between Japan and its major trading partners, particularly the United States. In other words, it might be argued that they ran Japan rather too well and against their own long-term interests.

These policies included urging leading American companies such as Motorola to buy Japanese-made products and cultivate special relationships with Japanese suppliers even if they were not perceived to abide by the same standards. But many factors are at play here. For example, Japan's economic recovery was also fueled by increased investment as a direct result of the Korean War* in the early 1950s. This was in part due to the fact that the war in Korea, which was fought along the ideological fault lines of the Cold War,* intensified the American desire to integrate Japan into the Western trading bloc, thereby protecting it from the Soviet Union.* Thus, Americans had specific strategic interests in rebuilding the Japanese economy.

The other major factor that characterized this particular era was globalization*—the worldwide movement toward more integrated economies, finance, trade, and communications that intensified in the 1980s. A new competitive environment emerged, leading to an increasing academic interest in both management strategy and understanding this new business model.

NOTES

1   Adrian Wooldridge, "The Guru at the Bottom of the Pyramid," *The Economist*, April 22, 2010.

2   C. K. Prahalad and Gary Hamel, "The Core Competence of the Corporation," *Harvard Business Review* 68, no. 3 (1990): 79.

3   Gary Hamel, "Gary Hamel," accessed March 20, 2015, http://www.garyhamel.com/.

4   Eiji Takemae, *Inside GCHQ: The Allied Occupation of Japan and Its Legacy*, trans. Robert Ricketts and Sebastian Swann (New York: Continuum, 2002).

ACADEMIC CONTEXT

KEY POINTS

- The discipline of business strategy,* by which a business implements a plan with the aim of achieving specific goals such as profit, growth, or market dominance, emerged out of economic theory.

- Prahalad and Hamel popularized a resource-based* approach to strategic management* (that is, an approach designed to make use of the resources unique to a business—its people and technology, for example—as it develops its strategy).

- The traditional view was that sales were the only driver for strategic management.

The Work in its Context

Strategy* can be traced to the ancient writings of the Chinese general Sun Tzu, but emerged as a business concept in the early 1900s. Prior to this, strategy was primarily something used by the military to devise offensive and counteroffensive moves. An early application of strategy to business thinking was Frederick Winslow Taylor's* *The Principles of Scientific Management*, published in 1911, which presented the idea that a business should make workers and their processes as efficient as possible.[1] Specifically, Taylor argued that efficiency lay in creating systematic procedures, not in finding unusually gifted employees. Taylor's ideas were highly influential and helped to promote strategy as a field of study and a practical tool. In 1931, the first executive education program was founded at the Massachusetts Institute of Technology, signaling that strategy was starting to be considered a viable and important part of a business leader's toolkit.

> ❝ The new terms of competitive engagement cannot be understood using analytical tools devised to manage the diversified corporation of 20 years ago, when competition was primarily domestic … and all the key players were speaking the language of the same business schools and consultancies. ❞
>
> C. K. Prahalad and Gary Hamel, "The Core Competence of the Corporation"

In the mid-1900s, corporations started to be structured around the notion of strategic business units.* An example is General Electric, which has housed businesses ranging from oil and gas to healthcare to aviation. The basic idea at that time was that strategy could be set for each individual business unit with its own clearly defined products and markets.

In the early 1960s a flurry of authoritative works catapulted the idea of strategy from something that was obscure and primarily of interest to academics to an important concern for business managers. This was largely due to the fact that research became more focused on understanding the challenges faced by business and how business reacted to these challenges. One notable example of strategy scholarship during this time was Bruce Henderson's* work on the "experience curve," which describes the idea that as companies have more experience in a market, their costs fall.[2] The analytic style of Henderson's work was emulated by many strategy scholars, including Prahalad and Hamel.

Overview of the Field

In the 1980s, expanding globalization* and competition motivated an increasing amount of strategic research on understanding what actually drove competitive advantage*—or the qualities and abilities that allow a business to out-compete its rivals. Initially this was based on traditional economic theory such as the need to understand product markets and industry structures. For example, this period saw a marked increase in the diversification* of corporations; that is, extending business activities into disparate fields, activities, or market sectors. The theory behind this is that such diversification offers a broader scope, which in turn reduces vulnerabilities to change or losses to any one business. Product differentiation,* by which a business tailors its product to be distinctive in a particular market, was also described in economic terms as "the degree of cost–price* inelasticity" with respect to competing brands[3] and as being "concerned with the bending of demand to the will of supply."[4] In other words, businesses were seeking new ways of distinguishing their products from competitors in order to be less vulnerable to shifts in demand.

Indeed, the basic economic idea of diversification suggests that a broader portfolio* of businesses or product lines improves the position of the business unit by having more options and lower vulnerabilities than any one business or product line. Competitive strategies were said to arise from minimizing transaction costs (making production as efficient as possible) or achieving economies of scale and scope (producing enough volume to significantly lower the cost of each unit sold). Because of these strategic goals, the focus for businesses was on the external environment, including economic conditions, allocation of resources, and competitor behavior.

In the late 1980s, however, there emerged the idea that internal resources—a business's staff and technology, for example—were themselves an unacknowledged source of substantial competitive advantage. This is where the work of Prahalad and Hamel sits, specifically with respect to the development of unique competencies acquired through the accumulation of knowledge and collective learning.

The resource-based view of strategy is concerned with both tangible and intangible resources, and is grounded in two assumptions: resources must differ between companies—if they were *all* the same then companies could not, logically speaking, out-compete each other; resources tend not to be mobile and do not move easily from company to company, at least not in the short term—for example, this assumption would be violated if a single employee moving from one company to another could bring with her all the significant resources of the original company. Due to this immobility, companies cannot replicate competitors' resources and implement the same strategies.

In summary, the traditional strategic management view was that the external environment provided the impetus for developing competitive advantage. Prahalad and Hamel popularized the little-known, resource-based approach that competitive advantage actually resulted from the internal environment and the internal resources available to the company.

Academic Influences

With strategy a young and rapidly evolving business discipline at the time, C. K. Prahalad and Gary Hamel would have been influenced by their peers.

The term "strategic management" was introduced into the business vocabulary in 1965 by Russian American mathematician and business scholar H. Igor Ansoff.* His ideas were further developed by Michael Porter,* perhaps one of the best-known strategy theorists from Harvard Business School. A major theme of Porter's work was the concept of competitive strategy and competitive advantage.

Strategic management ideas that influenced Prahalad and Hamel also came from American economist David Teece* and his work on dynamic capabilities. The ability to build and adapt competencies to address rapidly changing environments has been considered as the best explanation for competitive advantages. But resolving issues of measuring and managing these competitive advantages led Prahalad and Hamel to develop the concept of "core competencies." This, in turn, resulted in "The Core Competence of the Corporation."

American business scholar Jay Barney* was also influential. He popularized the "resource view" of the corporation. This view says that resources must also be analyzed and understood in developing a corporate strategy. Here the internal environment was seen to be as important as the external environment.

There were also certain institutions that influenced Prahalad and Hamel. Both men were products of the Ross School of Business at the University of Michigan, which had a reputation for producing graduates with practical leanings. Their programs developed students' professional and practical skills, and provided them with the ability to turn knowledge and ideas into practice. It was this approach to their work that contributed to Prahalad and Hamel's stellar careers, both as co-researchers and later on their own.

NOTES

1   A. T. Kearney. *The History of Strategy and Its Future Prospects* (Chicago: A. T. Kearney Inc., 2014), 3.

2   A. T. Kearney, *History of Strategy*, 3.

3   Michael E. Porter, *Interbrand Choice, Strategy and Bilateral Market Power* (Cambridge, MA: Harvard University Press, 1976).

4   Wendell Smith, "Product Differentiation and Market Segmentation as Alternative Marketing Strategies," *Journal of Marketing* 21, no. 1 (1956): 3–8.

MODULE 3
THE PROBLEM

KEY POINTS

- Setting down their ideas, Prahalad and Hamel sought to identify the factors that afford corporations competitive advantage.*

- The traditional view of competitive advantage emphasized universal market conditions and the international political environment.

- Prahalad and Hamel argued that, in fact, competitive advantage was derived from the combination of a business's knowledge and resources.

Core Question

C. K. Prahalad and Gary Hamel's "The Core Competence of the Corporation" seeks to address specific questions about how a business might best use its available resources to become competitive.

Competitive advantage is not a new subject. The control of cost, product differentiation* (tailoring a product to be distinctive in the market), and market segmentation* (by which a business targets subsections of a given market with shared interests) have always mattered in business. But research tended to cover marketing, production, finance, control, and other activities that have a well-attested role in arriving at competitive advantage. All these needed to be put together.

In the 1980s, however, American business was challenged by the growing forces of globalization,* antitrust laws* (laws designed by the American government to protect consumers from predatory business practices), and high inflation. Internally, management purely focused on financial performance rather than on operations.[1]

> **❝** Prahalad and Hamel succeeded in persuading managers to look at strategy as something fluid and imprecise … It was a switch from the more modular approach of Michael Porter and of the tradition of scientific management. Porter had turned strategic thinking back in the direction of Frederick Taylor; Prahalad and Hamel changed that direction by several degrees. **❞**
>
> *The Economist*, "Core Competence"

Until the 1980s, business focused on how industries were structured and on analyzing the competition. This was to become known as "comparative advantage"* (the ability of an organization to carry out a particular economic activity more efficiently than another organization) to differentiate it from "competitive advantage" (an advantage that an organization has allowing it to generate greater sales or margins or retain more customers than its competition). Since then, questions of how to plan for the future and how to build companies that could withstand rapidly changing business conditions using internal know-how became fully integrated into the strategy process.

The Participants

Three academics are credited with being founders of business strategy* as a discipline. They are the Russian American mathematician and business strategist H. Igor Ansoff,* the American business historian Alfred D. Chandler,* and the American business scholar Kenneth R. Andrews.*[2]

Ansoff's *Corporate Strategy*[3] was the first "how to" strategy book. For Ansoff, traditional ideas of planning and budgeting were no longer fit for purpose; business needed to think and imagine more, and developing strategy was a question of anticipating future challenges and tests.

Chandler thought the "visible hand" of management should replace the "invisible hand" of market forces. He called this the "managerial revolution."[4]

Andrews, meanwhile, developed the SWOT* pattern of strategy analysis—the strategic analysis of *strengths, weaknesses, opportunities,* and *threats.*[5] His idea was that "competitive advantage" is achieved by "implementing strategies that exploit their inner strengths … and avoiding internal weaknesses."[6]

These three ideas were all predicated on top-down management. They all signally failed to actually define a corporation's quite unique competitive advantage—if indeed there was one.

The business scholars Henry Mintzberg* and James Waters* saw strategy emerging from actions and behaviors at various levels within an organization.[7] The fundamental difference between deliberate and emergent strategy*—Mintzberg's term for a business strategy that emerged as a response to events—was that a *deliberate* strategy focused on control while an emergent strategy allowed for flexibility, responsiveness, and a willingness to learn. For Mintzberg and Waters, taking the latter route was a better fit in an increasingly complex, uncertain, and changing environment.

The resource-based view* focuses on the internal, individual characteristics of an organization. The American business scholar Jay Barney* distinguished between tangible resources (machinery and land, for example) and intangible resources (intellectual resources, patents, knowledge, and so on), and human and non-human internal resources. He suggested that, by making it easier to align organizational activity with employee performance requirements, human resource management becomes a means for developing unique resources that can be considered building blocks of competitive advantage.

The Contemporary Debate

Management theorists and strategists traditionally had the following view—either a product had to be offered at a lower price than competitors' products or the product had to have unique benefits that possibly justified a higher price. The business scholar Michael Porter* devised two basic types of competitive advantage: "cost leadership"* (an economic term meaning the lowest cost of operation in the industry) and "differentiation."[8]

Focusing on corporate *structure* meant that competitive advantage was largely driven by external factors such as financing, competitors, markets, and people. This kind of strategy responded to the environment and opportunity. Prahalad and Hamel, however, thought businesses should all look within to gain insights into their own future. Although their idea may be superficially similar to a traditional resource-based approach, in truth it was very different indeed, focusing on very different kinds of resources.

Prahalad and Hamel do not explicitly acknowledge any other schools of thought in the work, and if the influence of their peers can be detected—they were not working, of course, in a vacuum—they never specifically address it. They distanced themselves, for example, from the then modish tendency to regard "strategy" as mainly defined by an external business and market environment.

They would not have been able to formulate their theory if it were not for their own practical fieldwork.

NOTES

1   Ram Charan and R. Edward Freeman, "Planning for the Business Environment of the 1980s," *Journal of Business Strategy* 1, no. 2 (1980): 9–19.

2   Gary Hamel and C. K. Prahalad, "Strategic Intent," *Harvard Business Review* 67, no. 3 (1989): 61; Anne S. Huff and Rhonda K. Reger, "A Review of Strategic Process Research," *Journal of Management* 13, no. 2 (1987): 211; Peter McKiernan, "Strategy Past; Strategy Futures," *Long Range Planning* 30, no. 5 (1997): 791.

3   H. Igor Ansoff, *Corporate Strategy: An Analytical Approach to Business Policy for Growth and Expansio*n (New York: McGraw-Hill, 1965).

4   Alfred Chandler, *The Visible Hand: The Managerial Revolution in American Business* (Cambridge, MA: Harvard University Press, 1977).

5   Kenneth R. Andrews, *The Concept of Corporate Strategy* (Homewood, IL: Richard D. Irwin, 1971).

6   Jay Barney, "Firm Resources and Sustained Competitive Advantage," *Journal of Management* 17, no. 1 (1991): 99.

7   Henry Mintzberg and James A. Waters, "Of Strategies, Deliberate and Emergent," *Strategic Management Journal* 6, no. 3 (1985): 257–72.

8   Michael Porter, *Competitive Advantage: Creating and Sustaining Superior Performance* (New York: Free Press, 1985), 3.

MODULE 4
THE AUTHORS' CONTRIBUTION

KEY POINTS

- A corporation's competitive advantage* is determined by its "core competencies"*—roughly, the knowledge, skills, and technologies that offer it a unique advantage over its rivals.

- Group-learned knowledge and skills are vital to the development of a business's strategy.*

- "The Core Competence of the Corporation" built on Prahalad and Hamel's previous research.

Authors' Aims

With "The Core Competence of the Corporation," C. K. Prahalad and Gary Hamel seek to persuade managers to view strategy* as coming from *within* their organization rather than something to be decided by outside forces and dynamics. Great strategies, they argue, can come from challenging a status quo.

Asserting that pre-existing assumptions should always be questioned, Prahalad and Hamel introduced the concept of "core competencies" as an innovative approach to creating corporate strategy. This also built on "strategic intent," an idea they had presented a year previously in a *Harvard Business Review** article. In the article, itself titled "Strategic Intent," Prahalad and Hamel set out their vision of strategic management* as one of developing a long-term purpose and goals; "The Core Competence of the Corporation" discusses how to get there. It was a call to examine the process itself, rather than just facts and figures.

> ❝ The critical task for management is to create an organization capable of infusing products with irresistible functionality or, better yet, creating products that customers need but have not yet even imaged … it requires radical change in the management of major companies. It means, first of all, that top managements of Western companies must assume responsibility for competitive decline. ❞
>
> C. K. Prahalad and Gary Hamel, "The Core Competence of the Corporation"

"The Core Competence of the Corporation" can even be seen as a how-to guide. The article contains a flowchart depicting the relationships between competencies, core products, and end products. It sets out three tests to be applied to identify core competencies in a company and also includes, rather counterintuitively, a section on "how not to think of competence."[1] Interestingly, Prahalad and Hamel do not *specifically* use the words "leadership" and "corporate culture"* (the vision and principles that members of an organization subscribe to that help define their collective identity). But we can assume that this is what they refer to when they write of cultivating a core competency "mind-set."

Approach

In writing "The Core Competence of the Corporation," C. K. Prahalad and Gary Hamel gathered their information from studying the operations of large corporations in the 1980s. They were intrigued by a prevailing issue of their time, and wanted to find some answers. That issue was this: Japanese companies were soundly beating European and US ones in almost every way. Why?

The Japanese were continually creating new products and finding new markets. Honda, for example, diversified from cars and motorcycles into lawn mowers and boats. Western companies faced increased competition from low-cost, high-quality Japanese imports. According to Prahalad and Hamel, the reason why Western companies were slow to react actually had nothing to do with managerial ability or technological capacity. Western companies, they found, would not see what was right in front of them—a goldmine of collective knowledge sitting in offices downstairs from the boardroom. They coined the term "core competence" to describe this.

Writing for a business audience, Prahalad and Hamel take a practical approach, employing case studies—a form of research used extensively in the social sciences and described by the social scientist Robert Yin* in his work *Case Study Research: Design and Methods* as an empirical inquiry (that is, a method of making scientific deductions based on observable evidence).[2]

Contribution in Context

Prahalad and Hamel note that the typical Western company had a corporate structure made up of a portfolio* of businesses—the collection of the products, services, and achievements of the company that creates its presence in the market. These businesses were related in terms of the products they put to market. The autonomy of these businesses was considered sacrosanct by those who managed them, and they operated with a system of trade-offs with and against each other. But Eastern companies, they note, preferred to develop a bedrock of expertise from which products naturally evolved.

They call for a management rethink; instead of focusing on separate units and becoming obsessed with day-to-day sales, they propose, a corporation's strategic solutions must come from within the same organization. Competitive advantage requires something distinctive, even special: a "core competence"—what the business scholar Peter Drucker,* a man described as "the inventor of management," referred to in 1964 when he asked, "What is our excellence?"[3]

"The Core Competence of the Corporation" continued previous collaborations between Prahalad and Hamel. Their major contribution to strategic management began with the paper "Strategic Intent" in 1989. Here, they argued that in order to achieve the greatest success, companies needed to improve their understanding of what they did and what they wanted. They also needed to differentiate between strategic fit (formulating strategy between portfolios, products, market niches, and customers) and strategic intent (which, they alleged, focuses more on strategic challenges than on financial targets).

Gaining a competitive advantage involved leveraging resources rather than curtailing them because company resources seemed finite. "The Core Competence" was not the last word from these pioneers, since both carried on expanding their ideas, sometimes on their own and sometimes teaming up again (as they did, for example, in the book *Competing for the Future*). The contributions made by Prahalad and Hamel have changed the world of strategic management forever.

NOTES

1   C. K. Prahalad and Gary Hamel, "The Core Competence of the Corporation," *Harvard Business Review* 68, no. 3 (1990): 82.

2   Robert K. Yin, *Case Study Research: Designs and Methods* (Thousand Oaks, CA: Sage, 1984).

3   Peter F. Drucker, *Managing for Results: Economic Tasks and Risk-Taking Decisions* (London: Heinemann, 1964), 227–9.

SECTION 2
IDEAS

MODULE 5
MAIN IDEAS

KEY POINTS

- Formulating a successful strategy* requires business managers to focus inside their organizations to identify its particular "competencies"—strengths, notably that of knowledge.

- For Prahalad and Hamel, "core competencies"* were like the healthy, deep roots of a tree, which nourish and stabilize the corporate structure—the trunk and branches everyone else can see.

- Their strategy is clear: rethink the corporate structure; create value.

Key Themes

In "The Core Competence of the Corporation," C. K. Prahalad and Gary Hamel challenge the concept of a corporation as being an amalgam of smaller business units. Instead of a portfolio* (a suite) of businesses managed independently as subdivisions of a particular business, they advocate a "portfolio of competencies" which spans *across* individual businesses. They challenge the concept of a corporation being nothing more than the sum of its parts and judged solely on the price and perception of their product. Although this was in essence a theoretical idea, Prahalad and Hamel use practical examples to illustrate the way they think about corporate management.

Prahalad and Hamel coined the term "core competencies" to designate the sum of an organization's knowledge about the best way to coordinate skills and technologies, and so on. They argue that core competencies are the real source of an organization's competitive

> **❝** Only if the company is conceived as a hierarchy of core competencies, core products, and market-focused business units will it be fit to fight. **❞**
>
> C. K. Prahalad and Gary Hamel, "The Core Competence of the Corporation"

advantage* since, by focusing on competencies, a corporation could adapt more quickly to changing conditions. The idea also encouraged corporations to develop products that are unique and inspire customer loyalty.

Comparing Western and Eastern corporations, particularly those of the United States and Japan, the authors note the willingness of Japanese corporations to create alliances in order to acquire competencies cheaply. The authors maintain that adherence to the traditional view of a corporation as a freight-train of individual units, or "portfolio of businesses," inhibits the ability of US corporations to fully exploit their own unacknowledged inner capabilities. Individual units should not pool and hoard their discoveries of best practice; they should freely distribute them across the entire corporation.

Prahalad and Hamel also introduce the new idea of a "strategic architecture,"* which they conceive of as a road map to the future. Constructing a strategic architecture requires the identification and development of core competencies with the aim of building a competitive advantage (something that one business has that another does not that will, ultimately, make a difference in the market). Although the terms are not used specifically by the authors, strategic architecture embodies both leadership and corporate culture,* both essential to a successful corporation.

Exploring the Ideas

For Prahalad and Hamel, the very essence of strategy and competitive advantage lies in the organic concept of core competencies. Western and US management need to rethink the whole idea of the "corporation." Instead of allowing units within the company to maximize sales at any cost, a coherent, self-reflective culture needs to be developed across all branches of an organization.

Indeed, Prahalad and Hamel describe their model of a corporation as a tree. The trunk and limbs symbolize core products while the leaves, flowers, and fruits represent end products. For example, Honda's expertise in engines is a core product. The motorbike or lawn mower they put specific engines into is the end product. It is the root system of the core competencies—in this example, Honda's constantly evolving internal knowledge about how to build great engines—that nourishes, sustains, and stabilizes the tree against the cold winter months and summer storms. But the use of the tree analogy shows how core competencies, core products, and end products are all linked. The value is that creating dominance in core products allows the corporation the ability to shape the evolution of products.

To make it clear to business managers what they considered core competencies might be, they laid down three clear tests to identify a core competence:
- it enables the creation of new products and new markets;
- it provides the customer with something they cannot get elsewhere;
- it is difficult for competitors to copy.

A product developed through a properly functioning core competence is, then, competitively unique; nothing else in the marketplace is really like it. Although a "competence," is not the same as a "core competence," it can *become* a core competence after suitable attention and investment.

As well as clearly defining a means for identifying what is, and what is not, a core competence, the authors refined the definition with some further observations. Core competencies span both portfolios *and* products. In other words, competencies inhabit all aspects of an organization. Core competencies should be more stable and evolve more slowly than products. Products are essentially the physical and temporary expression of a corporation's core competencies. Only continual work creates and develops core competencies. Market competition, at the level of visible products, is only the surface expression of the true battle—a battle fought with the core competencies of organizations in competition.

Language and Expression

Prahalad and Hamel were writing for a business management audience. As strategic managers themselves, and having practical corporate experience, they would most likely have understood that their ideas could only be accepted and implemented if they were properly understood. And so their analyses of companies were turned into case studies. This allowed them the freedom to demonstrate their ideas and concepts with practical examples.

The text is not so much about determining the *content* of strategy, but rather the *process* of strategy. It is a practical argument stressing the importance of identifying a corporation's core competencies. Prahalad and Hamel achieved this by using examples of large, well-known organizations including Honda, Sony, and Canon. It drives home the point that it is these core competencies that provide a corporation's competitive advantage, because this is what distinguishes a corporation from its competition. And so they are important in creating strategy.

The article is insightful, informative, and challenging. Prahalad and Hamel use comparative cases to understand the changing basis for leadership and to make the case for real changes in the role of management, the development of strategy, and the concept of management strategy. The practical examples of corporations that are used allow the reader to follow their arguments logically. Practical examples show the practical application of their concepts, and the analogy of the tree makes it easy to grasp their point.

MODULE 6
SECONDARY IDEAS

KEY POINTS

- Prahalad and Hamel advocated overarching strategic architecture;* this requires the identification of core competencies* to build a structure useful for putting a strategy* in place.

- Strategic architecture replaces the traditional notion of a strategic plan.

- While the idea is introduced in "The Core Competence of the Corporation," the concept is future developed in subsequent articles.

Other Ideas

The material for "The Core Competence of the Corporation" was amassed from data gathered by C. K. Prahalad and Gary Hamel from large organizations.

They noticed that in corporate structures in which the arms of the business were separated, those business units, as they are known, tended to operate in isolation from each other. Only the act of applying for capital—that is, money that might be used in investment—united them. In other words, the only connection these portfolios* had to other areas of the company was access to the same pool of internal capital. New opportunities were neither explored nor developed. They refer to this as "the tyranny of the strategic business unit."* Because creating, developing, and utilizing core competencies involves working across every business unit making up an organization, they realized, a different structural form was required.

> ❝ Constructing strategic architecture requires conscious attention to developing mechanisms for organizational learning, innovation and experimentation, constructive contention, empowerment, optimized value potential, corporate sustainability, and strategic re-framing. Firms with a thoughtful and durable commitment to these meta-strategies will not only survive to see the next century, they are likely to dominate it. ❞
>
> Matthew J. Kiernan, "The New Strategic Architecture: Learning to Compete in the Twenty-First Century"

In order for organizations to be more successful, Prahalad and Hamel developed what they termed "strategic architecture." Building this was a question of identifying which competencies needed to be developed and which technologies, staffing, and other resources were required to create competitive advantages* in the future. All resources, not capital alone, needed to be available everywhere in the company without favor. Key employees should be weaned off the idea that they belonged to one particular area or business unit of the organization.

Strategic architecture has come to mean the way in which a business *comes together.* This allows the proper deployment of resources to wherever they are most needed within the organization—whether these be financial, staff-led, or simply ways of doing things. A long-term view of how an organization will grow, strategic architecture is central to the development of a successful strategy.

Exploring the Ideas

By using the case studies of the Vickers Group and Honda, Prahalad and Hamel show how the task of creating strategic architecture "forces the organization to identify and commit to the technical and production linkages across [strategic business units] that will provide a distinct competitive advantage."[1] The idea of strategic architecture, introduced in "The Core Competence of the Corporation" and developed in their 1996 work *Competing for the Future*, is especially useful in that it replaces the traditional bald strategic plan.

In "The Core Competence," Prahalad and Hamel refer to the US technology company NEC in 1990 as "the world leader in semiconductors and … a first-tier player in telecommunications products and computers" with US \$3.8 billion in sales.[2] In *Competing for the Future*, the authors show that, by identifying and implementing three streams of technological and market evolution, this strategic architecture enabled NEC to produce US \$26.2 billion in sales in 1992.[3]

In a separate article in 1993, Prahalad refers to strategic architecture as a framework for leveraging corporate resources. It is a "distillation of a wide variety of information."[4]

Overlooked

In "The Core Competence of the Corporation," Prahalad and Hamel demonstrate that successful corporations are able to enter new, even unrelated, businesses as a direct consequence of their core competencies. Once again, competitive advantage is helped by collective wisdom grown organically within a company. That said, it is not entirely clear that simply by having these core competencies a business has an automatic advantage that will seamlessly translate into sales. What may be equally important, even if not actually mentioned by Prahalad and Hamel, are raw capabilities.

This is best illustrated by revisiting the Honda example from "The Core Competence." In it, Prahalad and Hamel attribute Honda's successful, swift move from motorcycles to cars, lawn mowers, and outboard motors to its underlying competence in the design and manufacture of engines. But core competencies alone cannot account for the speed at which a corporation can successfully move into other businesses.

What Honda had that its competitors such as General Motors lacked was expertise in *dealer management*, specifically with respect to training and support, covering *all* sales aspects from selling to servicing. Honda also had an internal structure that was different from its competitors. Instead of planning, testing, and building prototypes as one separate process following another, Honda ran them all at the same time, allowing them to make variations to the product lines more easily and cost effectively.

Honda's core competencies were its competitive advantage—but competencies and capabilities are not the same. Core competence is about technological and production expertise viewed from an internal perspective; capability is much broader, encompassing both internal and external aspects of the value chain (the sequence of activities a business performs as it brings a valuable product to market). If you include "capabilities" in the equation of success, it is fairly obvious that "core competencies" cannot, on their own, be a magic formula. Corporate strategy must be multidimensional.

The idea that capabilities were associated with competitive advantage can be attributed to the Berkeley economics professor David Teece,* Harvard Business School's Gary Pisano,* and the Silicon Valley economist Amy Shuen* in their 1997 article "Dynamic Capabilities and Strategic Management."[5] The argument was further developed by David Teece[6] over the following 10 years.

Despite these key assessments from the late 1990s, it is only really in the last few years that the two ideas have been put together.[7] Because the two concepts do actually complement each other, however, it is unlikely to have a significant effect on how "The Core Competence of the Corporation" is considered.

Macat Analysis of **C. K. Prahalad and Gary Hamel's**
The Core Competence of the Corporation

NOTES

1   C. K. Prahalad and Gary Hamel, "The Core Competence of the Corporation," *Harvard Business Review* 68, no. 3 (1990): 89.

2   Prahalad and Hamel, "The Core Competence of the Corporation," 79.

3   C. K. Prahalad and Gary Hamel, *Competing for the Future* (Boston, MA: Harvard Business Review Press, 1996).

4   C. K. Prahalad, "The Role of Core Competencies in the Corporation," *Research Technology Management* 36, no. 6 (1993): 43.

5   David J. Teece et al., "Dynamic Capabilities and Strategic Management," *Strategic Management Journal* 18, no. 17 (1997): 509–33.

6   David J. Teece, "Explicating Dynamic Capabilities: The Nature and Foundations of (Sustainable) Enterprise Performance," *Strategic Management Journal* 28, no. 13 (2007): 1319–50.

7   See, for example, J. H. Lim et al., "Role of IT Executives in the Firm's Ability to Achieve Competitive Advantage through IT Capability," *International Journal of Accounting Information Systems* 13, no. 1 (2012): 21–40; F. S. Nobr et al., *Technological, Managerial and Organizational Core Competencies: Dynamic Innovation and Sustainable Development* (Hershey, PA: IGI Global, 2012).

ACHIEVEMENT

KEY POINTS

- "The Core Competence of the Corporation" showed business managers developing a corporate strategy how to identify core competencies* in order to develop a competitive advantage* in the marketplace.

- Prahalad and Hamel's ideas were based on practical case studies backed up by rigorous academic studies.

- There is no one-size-fits-all method: every company is different and so the process of identifying core competencies will always differ.

Assessing the Argument

Although published in 1990, "The Core Competence of the Corporation" by C. K. Prahalad and Gary Hamel is still widely admired within the business community. Written in reaction to an era of increasing globalization* (that is, ever-more integrated trade, economies, finance, and communication across the globe), and the rise of large corporations, the ideas advanced focused on process rather than determining the content of strategy.

This focus on process allows organizations to tailor their implementation of Prahalad and Hamel's thought while nevertheless adhering to the set of standard principles that they propose; the way in which they approached their work resulted in a practical discussion on creating strategy.

The article was written specifically for business managers rather than academics. Good use is made of case studies to portray both the issues and the potential solutions. It was only after it was apparent that

> ❝ When we consider both Apple and Google, it is clear that multiple core competencies are abundant within both organizations, driving their value, stock price and putting them way ahead of even the strongest multinational businesses. ❞
>
> The Marketing People, "Apple Maps Vs. Google Maps and the Importance of Core Competencies in Strategy"

the ideas appealed to the business community that the core concepts were further explored and developed outside of business. This is not to say that the ideas were not rooted in academic or scientific rigor; strategic management* generally, and competitive advantage in particular, had been discussed and debated and were therefore not novel ideas. What Prahalad and Hamel did with these subjects was, however, innovative.

Achievement in Context

It takes time for new ideas to get absorbed into business—especially given the challenges of international competition brought about by globalization and the fact that corporate structure was seen by some as the one fixed and unchangeable thing in a changeable world. So we can consider Prahalad and Hamel's warning of "the tyranny of the SBU"—that is, the strategic business unit, the autonomous components of a business responsible for their own products and profits—to be striking.

Many of the case studies on which Prahalad and Hamel based their theories were large Japanese corporations. The assessments were made in the 1980s, but the performance of many of these corporations had become less impressive by the end of the century. However, it is important to note that, just because some of these Japanese businesses stalled in the late 1990s, this does not mean that it was as a direct, or even as an indirect, result of those aspects of their strategy that Prahalad and Hamel had praised. There would have been a number of contributing factors, notably coming from the *external* environment. The subsequent recovery of many of these organizations suggests that the underlying strategy was relatively sound.

The idea of "core competencies" was picked up and expanded on by other researchers of strategy. The new formulations have been described with different names; the economics and business scholars David Teece,* Gary Pisano,* and Amy Shuen* refer to "dynamic capabilities," for example, in their paper "Dynamic Capabilities and Strategic Management."[1] Other terms include "combinative," "distinctive," and "organizational" capabilities.[2]

Since the publication of "The Core Competence of the Organization," much research has been done to find real-world applications in the form of better services and better products; it seems that these things can make a critical contribution to corporate competitiveness.

Limitations

For Prahalad and Hamel, identifying and exploiting core competencies explained why some organizations worked better than others. They also homed in on the problem of an organization's different departments acting independently. This raises the very good question: If *all* organizations are continually trying to gain a competitive advantage over other organizations, why is a business "portfolio* strategy" model (according to which an organization is composed of semi-independent or even autonomous businesses) still followed today? It follows that there are many agents at play here; there is no one-size-fits-all approach to determining strategy.

It may even seem that the original analysis by Prahalad and Hamel has dated. Many of the companies held up at the time as shining examples of commercial success are now not quite so successful.[3]

There may be cultural aspects to all this, as different cultures embody distinctive behaviors and beliefs. The cultural expectation of a "job for life" is not universal. Both notions of outsourcing*—that is, contracting work out to a third party—and specialization have different responses from management in different parts of the world. Whatever the evolution in corporate strategy, these types of issues never go away. In looking for solutions to certain issues we return to the fields of corporate strategy, strategic management, and organizational learning (that is, roughly, the development of an organization's understanding of itself and the marketplace).

Core competencies are defined as the knowledge, skills, and resources embedded in an organization that together allow it to develop a product in a better way than their competitors. Leadership, however, defined by the business journal *Forbes* as "a process of social influence, which maximizes the efforts of others, towards the achievement of a goal,"[4] is important too. The leader's core competencies are also knowledge, emotional intelligence (EQ), and resources.

So the article's thesis is not applicable to big companies alone. The term "core competency" has also come to mean qualities or skills an individual possesses. The concept has been described as the "immediate predecessor to, and likely the driver of, the current surge of competency modeling practice"[5]—the exercise of addressing how business objectives are met and work is accomplished (a field associated with industrial and organizational psychology).

While Prahalad and Hamel did not specifically address human resource management,* they opened the door to the new idea that line managers (that is, people charged with administrative tasks directly associated with production) might play a more strategic and operational role in staff management.

NOTES

1   David Teece et al., "Dynamic Capabilities and Strategic Management," *Strategic Management Journal* 18, no. 17 (1997): 509–33.

2   Bruce Kogut and Udo Zander, "Knowledge of the Firm, Combinative Capabilities, and the Replication of Technology," *Organization Science* 3, no. 3 (1992): 383–97.

3   *The Economist*, "Core Competence," September 15, 2008.

4   K. Kruse, "What is Leadership," *Forbes*, April 9, 2013, accessed March 20, 2015, http://www.forbes.com/sites/kevinkruse/2013/04/09/what-is-leadership/.

5   Jeffrey S. Shippmann et al., "The Practice of Competency Modeling," *Personnel Psychology* 53, no. 3 (2000): 712.

MODULE 8
PLACE IN THE AUTHORS' WORK

KEY POINTS

- Both Prahalad and Hamel focus on leadership and innovation driven by management strategy.*

- While Hamel has continued to evolve the practice of management, Prahalad's attention, however, turned to how value is created.

- "The Core Competence of the Corporation" was one of a number of significant joint works that addressed the continuing need for ever-changing strategy.

Positioning

C. K. Prahalad and Gary Hamel's article "The Core Competence of the Corporation, founded on the question of what makes some corporations more successful than others, is the product of two business scholars interested in the strategic management* of corporations.

Hamel was particularly interested in challenging traditional strategic planning by promoting organizational innovation, and the article, which came at the beginning of his career, determined the path he was to follow: he would later go on to develop his own (revolutionary) style of strategic innovation. He has continually sought to evolve the practice of management.

Hamel pioneered new concepts of "industry revolution" and "management innovation" which have now changed the practice of management around the world. He also established the world's first "management lab" in California, where businesspeople and academics can work together to develop good practice and to consider how

> ❝ To compete successfully for the future, senior managers must first understand just how competition for the future is different from competition for the present. The differences are profound. They challenge the traditional perspectives on strategy and competition. Competing for the future requires not only a definition of strategy, but also a redefinition of top management's role in creating strategy. ❞
>
> Gary Hamel and C. K. Prahalad, *Competing for the Future*

business performance might be improved by rethinking organizational structure* (that is, the coordinated distribution of labor and management tasks designed to further an organization's objectives).

The US financial periodical *Wall Street Journal* ranks Hamel as the "world's most influential business thinker" and *Fortune* magazine calls him "the world's leading expert on business strategy." He is consistently listed in the world's top management thought leaders.[1]

Prahalad co-authored "The Core Competence of the Corporation" towards the middle of his career. After first publishing on the subject of healthcare management, he co-authored *The Multinational Mission: Balancing Local Demands and Global Vision* (1987) with the business strategist Yves Doz,* on themes of global competitiveness and corporate capabilities. He developed these ideas further in the joint publications with Hamel.

Prahalad was a natural collaborator by instinct and temperament, often leaving his colleague to continue developing a joint idea on their own. While still working broadly in the field of strategy he was already looking at startling new ideas such as how the world's poor could (counterintuitively) be a valuable market and ecological sustainability as a driver of business innovation. The founder of Microsoft, Bill Gates,* referred to this as fighting poverty with profitability.[2]

Prahalad was always true to his professed ideals. In a lecture first delivered to students in 1977 he outlined the duties of the "responsible manager." So much did this lecture truly and wholly represent his world view that he delivered it annually, word for word, for the next 33 years.

Integration

Prahalad and Hamel established their strategic management credentials in 1989 when they co-authored the paper "Strategic Intent." Traditional strategic management was a question of "strategic fit"—matching business portfolios,* market niches, and products, while emphasizing financial targets and resource constraints. In "Strategic Intent," Prahalad and Hamel introduced the concept of "core competencies" with respect to strategic leadership. A year later, in "The Core Competence of the Corporation," they argued that corporations cannot be defined by what they *do* but, rather, by what they *know*. This alone promotes business prowess.

Top-ranking companies, they argue, have a good sense of new business opportunities—a theme developed in the later book *Competing for the Future* (1994), which finally pulls together the ideas of "strategic intent," "strategic architecture," and "core competencies."

Both "Strategic Intent" and "The Core Competence of the Corporation" won Prahalad and Hamel the McKinsey Award*—an award made annually by the American consulting firm McKinsey & Company and the *Harvard Business Review** recognizing the best articles published in the journal. While they co-authored a total of 12 books and journal articles between 1983 and 1996, ultimately Prahalad and Hamel went their own ways, pursuing related interests.

Prahalad turned more and more to researching how "value" is created before returning to the field of core competencies in 2008 with the book *The New Age of Innovation: Driving Co-Created Value Through Global Networks*, in which he examined how companies can build capabilities to achieve and sustain continuous improvement and innovation.

For Hamel, evolving the practice of management is key. He developed his own style of "revolutionary strategic innovation," pioneering the concepts of "industry revolution" and "management innovation" which have changed the practice of management in corporations around the world.

He has not been without his critics, however. In one notorious act of ill-judgment, Hamel had held up the energy company Enron as an example of his style of revolutionary strategic innovation. A year later, in 2001, Enron collapsed in one of the worst corporate scandals of our times.

Although Hamel's reputation has never entirely recovered from this association, this does not detract from the brilliance of his early pioneering work. In 2007 he published *The Future of Management* in which he declared that "management is out of date."[3]

Significance

C. K. Prahalad and Gary Hamel co-authored twelve texts between 1983 and 1996 of which "The Core Competence of the Corporation" published in 1990 was the fifth. Of other works the most significant are "Strategic Intent" (1989), "Strategy as Stretch and Leverage" (1993), and *Competing for the Future* (1994); all are interrelated. The author's reputations are not built on any one single text but, rather, on the contribution they make as a coherent and developing argument.

The exact significance of "The Core Competence" is not always obvious; references may date and change, and terminology may shift. But the basic ideas behind core competence and strategic architecture—among them leadership, management strategy, marketing, and human resources—underlie all sub-disciplines related to competitive advantage.*

Other sub-disciplines directly influenced by the discoveries of "The Core Competence" include organizational learning* (the creation and sharing of knowledge in an organization), knowledge management,* and corporate culture.* This stems from the emphasis Prahalad and Hamel placed on how to grow core competencies.

Business is not static. Its continual growth and evolution means that there is always a need to change and adapt. It is likely, then, that the text's significance will continue to evolve in coming years.

NOTES

1   Reported in Ruth Young, "Interview with Gary Hamel," *Strategic Direction* 25, no. 4 (2002): 30–1.

2   C. K. Prahalad, *The Fortune at the Bottom of the Pyramid* (Upper Saddle River, NJ: Prentice Hall, 2005).

3   Gary Hamel with Bill Breen, *The Future of Management* (Boston, MA: Harvard Business School Press, 2007), x.

SECTION 3
IMPACT

MODULE 9
THE FIRST RESPONSES

KEY POINTS

- Debate has centered on concepts and strategies more generally, rather than on Prahalad and Hamel's text specifically.

- It is argued that core competencies* alone are not enough to ensure competitive advantage* and that changes in international competition require different strategic approaches.

- Advances in technology and the shift to industries that provide services rather than manufactured products move the focus from organizational structures towards organizational psychology—the understanding of human psychology as it is expressed in behavior in the workplace.

Criticism

In "The Core Competence of the Corporation," C. K. Prahalad and Gary Hamel argue that sustainable competitive advantage resulted from the proper understanding of a business's unique *internal* environment (its resources and knowledge) rather than an understanding of how best to respond to the *external* environment (the market, for example, or a national economy).

The article was part of an array of literature on the subject of strategy* published in the late 1980s and early 1990s offering criticism of the multi-divisional organizational structure of corporations and their old-fashioned strategies based on portfolios.* This literature advocated the need to look within the organization to make best use of long-term competitive capabilities.

> ❝ But as the strategies piled up so did the complexity, and the chance that any one overall strategy was the answer to ever expanding strategic freedom was trampled in the competitive scramble. ❞
>
> A. T. Kearney, *The History of Strategy and Its Future Prospects*

As a result, little criticism was aimed at any specific text such as "The Core Competence of the Corporation." Nor was it personally aimed at authors such as Prahalad and Hamel. Business managers, management correspondents, and consultants raised the least criticism—possibly because Prahalad and Hamel wrote specifically for the business audience. Academic study, however, was a little harsher; for example, the text was criticized for making "no attempt at all" to conceptualize and assess the idea of core competencies in terms of economics.[1] And, because there had been a long history of studying these business ideas, it was suggested that Prahalad and Hamel had really invented almost nothing at all and had, rather, extrapolated from past practice and simply generalized.[2]

While Prahalad and Hamel argued that market positioning was a necessary part of the strategy for an organization, the journalists John Micklethwait* and Adrian Wooldridge* disputed this. They contend that being first to market is not a guarantee of success, and indeed many companies have benefitted from entering a market after the market leader.[3]

Moreover, the business consultants Michael Treacy* and Fred Wiersema* argue that the mere fact of having core competencies is not enough ensure success.[4] To support this contention they compare the Wisconsin engine-maker Briggs & Stratton with the Japanese titan Honda (used by Prahalad and Hamel as a case study in "The Core Competence of the Corporation"). They make the point that, although both companies have engineering competence, Briggs &

Stratton has not been nearly so successful—clearly, Honda's dominance comes from something else besides knowledge of engines.

Perhaps the most constructive criticism came from critics such as Shirish Srivastava,* associate professor at the HEC School of Management in Paris, who points out that although the development of a corporate-wide strategic architecture* is one of Prahalad and Hamel's fundamental messages, they do not explain how it should best be devised.

Responses

Globalization* and the formation of large complex organizational structures in the 1980s resulted in a mountain of new research into corporate strategy generally, and competitive advantage in particular. Prahalad and Hamel contributed to this debate through a number of articles of which "Strategic Intent" in 1989 and "The Core Competence of the Corporation" in 1990 were best known at the time. The latter in particular provided a practical approach to the adoption of a corporate strategy focused on the organization's internal environment.

Their debate on different approaches was healthy. In response to the argument that strategy is really about "positioning" a business in a given industry structure,[5] Prahalad and Hamel countered with the argument that "the reality of business during the 1990s is that industry structures are far from stable and are undergoing major transitions."[6] The core competency approach suggests that companies can withstand these transformations by building internal knowledge.

Their 1994 article "Strategy as a Field of Study: Why Search for a New Paradigm?" might be viewed as a response to their critics. In it, they state their belief that there is "turmoil in the field, in research and in practice" and that while "much of the criticism of the field may be valid, critics often miss the point."[7] Rather than conceding that shifting market conditions had downgraded the importance of strategy,

Prahalad and Hamel argue that strategic thinking, and specifically internally oriented strategic thinking, is even more vital in volatile markets.

Their criticism of their own critics is notably muted: "We believe that during the last 10 years (1984–94), competitive space has been dramatically altered … Why did this radical industry transformation, the contours of which were visible for some time, escape systematic and persistent attention from managers? It apparently escaped the attention of academics as well."[8]

Conflict and Consensus

Prahalad and Hamel were prolific authors, writing together and individually. Their subsequent works continued to build on ideas exploring corporate strategy, organizational structure,* and competitive advantage using the concepts first proposed in "The Core Competence of the Corporation." For example, the ideas regarding strategic architecture are only fully explored in their 1996 work *Competing for the Future*. Strategy, as a business discipline, was also broadened by their work.

If the 1990s were "strategy heydays" according to A.T. Kearney* (a global management consulting firm who specialize in advising corporations on strategic matters), the period from the mid-1990s to the mid-2010s was a time of "strategy proliferation."[9] Advances in technology and a shift from industrial-based to service-based economies helped to move the discussion in the field away from the subject of organizational structures towards organizational psychology—that is, towards the study of human behavior in the workplace.

This move towards people-centered approaches to management[10] was welcomed by other authors such as Daniel Levinthal* and Jennifer Myatt, who together argued that research on strategy had become too centered on the organization and industry dynamics were being ignored.[11]

The evolution of management strategy ensured the continual evolution of the ideas of Prahalad, Hamel, and their critics. Any modification of their views can be seen as a reasonable reaction to advances in the discipline rather than to a change of mind.

NOTES

1   Nicolai J. Foss, "Wither the Competitive Perspective?" in *Towards a Competence Theory of the Firm*, ed. Nicolai J. Foss and Christian Knudsen (London: Routledge, 1996).

2   Daniel W. Rasmus, "How Clinging to Core Competencies Is Breaking Your Organization's Heart," *Fast Company*, August 22, 2012.

3   John Micklethwait and Adrian Wooldridge, *The Witch Doctors: Making Sense of the Management Gurus* (New York: Times Books, 1996).

4   Michael Treacy and Fred Wiersema, *The Discipline of Market Leaders: Choose Your Customers, Narrow Your Focus, Dominate Your Market* (Reading, MA: Addison-Wesley, 1995).

5   The primary focus of Michael Porter's strategic analysis is the business unit. See M. E. Porter, *Competitive Strategy: Techniques for Analyzing Industries and Competitors* (New York: Free Press, 1980).

6   C. K. Prahalad and Gary Hamel, "Strategy as a Field of Study: Why Search for a New Paradigm?" *Strategic Management Journal Special Issue* 15 (1994): 10.

7   Prahalad and Hamel, "Strategy as a Field of Study," 6.

8   Prahalad and Hamel, "Strategy as a Field of Study," 6.

9   A. T. Kearney, *The History of Strategy and Its Future Prospects* (Chicago: A. T. Kearney Inc., 2014).

10 John Kay, *Foundations of Corporate Success: How Business Strategies Add Value* (Oxford: Oxford University Press, 1995).

11 Daniel Levinthal and Jennifer Myatt, "Co-Evolution of Capabilities and Industry: The Evolution of Mutual Fund Processing," *Strategic Management Journal* 15 (1994): 46.

MODULE 10
THE EVOLVING DEBATE

KEY POINTS

- "The Core Competence of the Corporation" highlighted the importance of the human factor in developing corporate strategy.

- Prahalad and Hamel's text changed the world of strategic management,* and popularized the resource-based* school of thought.

- Current researchers such as the French business thinker Thomas Durand* have taken up the idea of "core competencies."*

Uses and Problems

The main idea of "The Core Competence of the Corporation" is that organizations need to look within their internal structures for the source of true competitive advantage.*

The secondary idea concerns designing a "strategic architecture."* This is achieved by identifying which competencies should be developed, and which technology, staffing, and other resourcing is required, to create competitive advantages. The specific aim is to better connect the organization to its customers and markets. Since the publication of "The Core Competence," there have been several interesting developments in our knowledge of strategic management generally and corporate strategy in particular.

Of particular note are the Harvard Business School's Robert Kaplan* and the businessman David Norton* who developed the "balanced scorecard" and "strategy maps."[1] The balanced scorecard provides metrics for valuing customer relationships, internal business

> ❝ What is strategy? We can now complete the answer to this question. Strategy is creating fit among a company's activities. The success of a strategy depends on doing many things well—not just a few—and integrating among them. If there is no fit among activities, there is no distinctive strategy and little sustainability. Management reverts to the simpler task of overseeing independent functions, and operational effectiveness determines an organization's relative performance. ❞
>
> Michael E. Porter, "What is Strategy?"

processes, and learning and growth; this enables managers to align "business activities to the vision and strategy* of the organization, improving internal and external communications, and monitoring organization performance against strategic goals." A strategy map, like a strategic architecture, is a model of how an organization creates value.

McGill University professor Henry Mintzberg* further developed Prahalad and Hamel's ideas into what he called "emergent strategy."* This required collecting from all levels of management, even employees, their knowledge about their customer and supplier experiences, and what trends they were picking up on. For Mintzberg, companies must become learning organizations. This builds on his article written with James Waters, "Of Strategies Deliberate and Emergent."[2]

There are many more examples of how "The Core Competence of the Corporation" has been a global business game-changer. Harvard's Michael Beer* has argued that some of the most powerful change ideas in an organization come from managers working on real business problems which cut across departments, jointly solving the problem.[3] This is in line with Prahalad and Hamel's contention about how organizations are structured.

Schools of Thought

With the publication of "The Core Competence of the Corporation," C. K. Prahalad and Gary Hamel changed the world of strategic management. The discipline of strategic management is extremely broad. But this article, while falling within the domain of strategic management, has also contributed to a number of areas of research that may not necessarily be considered to be part of that field.

The most obvious of these is the concept of "organizational learning"* (the process by which knowledge is developed and shared throughout an organization). Much of the work in this area following Prahalad and Hamel's efforts has focused on understanding and measuring the knowledge of a corporation.

A number of schools of thought have developed from this famous article. The "capability-based" school argues that the source of competitive advantage is in competencies, for example a business's ability to bring a product to market faster than its competitors. For the "resource-based" school of strategic management, sustainable competitive advantage results from the knowledge, value-creating skills, and competencies derived from an organization's internal resources. These two schools are differentiated by how much emphasis they place on specific competencies versus the overall learning of the organization. "New games strategies"* is a contemporary school of thought that maintains competitive advantage is generated internally through innovation. This encompasses not only new products and services but also new processes and new ways of doing business.

In Current Scholarship

Organizational learning happens through the interaction between a number of business concepts such as structure, strategy, environment, technology, and culture. For Prahalad and Hamel, organizational learning was critical to the development of core competencies. Indeed, the term "core competence" was coined by them to represent the *collective learning* in an organization that gives it its competitive advantage. That is, those skills and attributes of the organization that set it apart from its competitors. This has led to "organizational learning" being the subject of huge interest and development, leading to many different sub-streams like transformation and change management. Another reason for the growth and diversity of this subject area is that there are very different understandings about the processes of organizational learning.

The idea of core competencies is centered on the concept of organizational learning. This, in itself, has been picked up and further studied or explored by other twenty-first-century researchers.[4] Professor Thomas Durand of the École Centrale in Paris took up the idea of a "competence portfolio,"* associating competence building and leveraging, or using something to its full potential.[5]

What does this mean? As the market changes, an organization may have to leverage its existing set of core competencies which, in turn, makes those very core competencies stronger. Durand, on the other hand, developed strategies to bridge the "competence gap."[6]

Prahalad and Hamel's "The Core Competence of the Corporation" has spawned widely diverse research. Their ideas have sparked not only new ideas, but also new ways of thinking.

NOTES

1   Robert S. Kaplan and David P. Norton, *The Balanced Scorecard: Translating Strategy into Action* (Boston, MA: Harvard Business Review Press, 1996).

2   Henry Mintzberg and James A. Waters, "Of Strategies, Deliberate and Emergent," *Strategic Management Journal* 6, no. 3 (1985): 257–72.

3   Karl Moore and Phil Lenir, "Mintzberg's Better Way to Do Corporate Strategy," *Forbes*, June 21, 2011.

4   These include Mary Crossan and Iris Bedrow, "Organizational Learning and Strategic Renewal," *Strategic Management Journal* 24, no. 11 (2003): 1087–105; Tuija Lehesvirta, "Learning Processes in a Work Organization: From Individual to Collective and/or Vice Versa?" *Journal of Workplace Learning* 16, no. 1/2 (2004): 92–100; M. Finger and S. B. Brand, *The Concept of the "Learning Organization" Applied to the Transformation of the Public Sector* (Thousand Oaks, CA: Sage, 1999); Mary Crossan et al., "An Organisational Learning Framework: From Intuition to Institution," *Academic Management Review* 24, no. 3 (1999): 522–37.

5   Thomas Durand, "Strategizing Innovation: Competence Analysis in Assessing Strategic Change," in *Competence-Based Strategic Management*, ed. Aimé Heene and Ron Sanchez (New York: John Wiley & Sons, 1997), 127–50.

6   Reported in Thomas Durand, "The Alchemy of Competence," in *Strategic Flexibility: Managing in a Turbulent Environment*, ed. Gary Hamel et al. (London: John Wiley & Sons, 1998), 303–30.

MODULE 11
IMPACT AND INFLUENCE TODAY

KEY POINTS

- Corporations face the same issues today that they faced in 1990; only the terminology has changed.
- Outsourcing,* re-engineering,* and transformation,* common terms today, all benefit from the idea of "core competencies."*
- The economic benefits of reduced costs can be achieved.

Position

C. K. Prahalad and Gary Hamel derived the material for their article "The Core Competence of the Corporation" from the analysis of a large number of organizations. While they assess predominantly Japanese and American corporations, the gap between which is today far less than some observers predicted in the 1980s and 1990s, their findings are still significant and relevant today especially with respect to the rapid growth of emerging economies in nations such as China, Brazil, India, Indonesia, Russia, and South Africa.

The idea of core competencies was further developed by other strategy* researchers. These subsequent authors sometimes used different terms to describe what would ultimately become known as "capability-based competitive advantage"*—that is, simply, advantages in the marketplace founded on a corporation's core competencies. The most common related expressions found in the relevant literature are "core skills," "organizational capabilities," "distinctive capabilities," "dynamic capabilities," and "organizational capital."

Since *The Core Competency of the Organization* was first published, research has brought into play a number of views as to what these

> **❝** But the real story is not about the number or size of the deals; it is about their character. Although some executives still use outsourcing primarily to offload non-core activities and reduce costs, many others have taken a much more sophisticated approach. Increasingly companies use outsourcing to gain access to competitive skills, improve service levels and increase their ability to respond to changing business needs. **❞**
>
> Jane C. Linder, Martin I. Cole, and Alvin J. Jacobson, "Business Transformation through Outsourcing"

"competencies" might possibly be (and how they can be applied to create better products and services). Combined with operational processes they can make a critical contribution to corporate competitiveness.

Today Prahalad and Hamel's approach to strategy is considered to be a "significant stream within the capability-based school."[1] Research on the sources of competitive advantage have all generally concluded that the more organizations follow the teachings of the capability-based school of thought, the greater their competitive advantage and the greater their performance.[2]

Interaction

In "The Core Competence of the Corporation," Prahalad and Hamel developed the concept of "core competencies"—the accumulated knowledge within an organization that serves as a source of competitive advantage. They developed the idea that competitive advantage is actively created by organizations through the accumulation of unique resources, capabilities, and knowledge.

The identification of "non-core" aspects of an organization as well as the idea of exploiting core competencies had led to the general idea of outsourcing—contracting non-core services out to third-party businesses. Management consultants were quick to pick up on this, encouraging companies to focus on core businesses as a source of growth and revenue potential (and to outsource everything else). Naturally, it did not take long for corporations to realize that competencies could be obtained from alternative sources such as contracting and franchising.

This allowed corporations to reduce employment levels. There was already a long history of criticism of such an approach.[3] Labor activists and trade unions thought "The Core Competence of a Corporation" "a cynical tactic of control adopted by management."[4]

But this is not all. The work's focus on core competencies in a competitive environment means that corporations must *continually* improve their practices. A new sub-industry of continuous improvement and lean management has evolved. The concepts or strategies of outsourcing, transformation, and lean management have, of course, been picked up on by academics who themselves have made substantial contributions to the intellectual debate, but the ideas mostly inhabit the business sector. A 2014 McKinsey & Company report describes the four principles of lean management as "delivering value efficiently to the customer," "enabling people to lead," "discovering better ways of working," and "connecting strategy, goals, and meaningful purpose."[5] The lean management approach is therefore closely related to the idea of building internal knowledge.

It is not known whether Prahalad and Hamel could have reasonably foreseen these applications. It could be said that practical application has actually distorted the original core ideas. But it is equally possible that economic developments have modified them.

There is another side to this, however, that makes the work possibly more important today than when they wrote it: people. The recognition of the strategic importance of human resources has put people at the heart of the concept of the core competence. An anecdotal example of this is the development of strong corporate cultures* at companies such as Google designed to attract, retain, and nurture excellent talent. As Felix Barber and Rainer Strack wrote in 2005, "It is no secret that business success today revolves largely around people, not capital."[6]

The Continuing Debate

Originally designed to illustrate to a puzzled audience of large Western (predominantly US) corporations why their counterparts in Asia were more profitable and more successful, developing core competencies became synonymous with creating global competitive advantage.

While the ideas sank in, international trade looked to outsourcing and offshoring (that is, employing people in cheap labor markets overseas to perform tasks that would be more expensive in wages at home). As such it had distinct political implications—basically, the promotion of free trade over domestic employment and protectionist policies (that is, the imposition of tariffs on imported goods with the aim of protecting domestic industry). At this international and political level, the idea of concentrating all one's efforts on what one does best—building core competencies—has been lost. It would seem that politics has distorted the purity of Prahalad and Hamel's original concept.

The financial industry has, consciously or otherwise, considered core competencies when working out whether to provide financial assistance. Business and economic events since the financial crises of 2007 to 2009—the effects of which are still being felt—have induced far-reaching changes in how businesses and capital markets behave. One of the more conspicuous changes has been in competitive behavior as organizations seek domination. Core competencies are seen as a straightforward business-performance measure and an indication of future success.[7]

This is a complex area of business strategy* and, while very much a business issue, it is certainly not confined to the business sector. It has wide-reaching consequences that have yet to be played out both domestically and on the world stage.

NOTES

1   T. Čater, "Capability-Based School of Thought's Relevance and Firms' Competitive Advantage Sources," *Zagreb International Review of Economics and Business* 7, no. 1 (2004): 40.

2   Čater, "Capability-Based School of Thought's Relevance," 54.

3   See, for example, K. Legge, *Power, Innovation and Problem Solving in Personnel Management* (Maidenhead: McGraw-Hill, 1978); K. M. Rowland and S. L. Summers, "Human Resource Planning: A Second Look," *Personnel Administration* 26, no. 12 (1981): 73–80.

4   M. Jabłoński, "The Methodology of Analyzing the Organization's Intellectual Capital," *Argumenta Oeconomica* 23, no. 2 (2009): 97–112.

5   McKinsey & Company, "The Lean Management Enterprise" (2014), accessed August 18, 2015 http://www.mckinsey.com/client_service/operations/latest_thinking/lean_management.

6   Felix Barber and Rainer Strack, "The Surprising Economics of a 'People Business,'" *Harvard Business Review* 83, no. 6 (2005): 80–90.

7   M. S. S. El Namaki, "Are We Seeing a Shift in Corporate Strategy Behaviour Today?" *Ivey Business Journal September/October* (2012): 1–4.

WHERE NEXT?

KEY POINTS

- "The Core Competence of the Corporation" will be relevant as long as there are corporations seeking competitive advantages.*

- The concepts of core competencies* and strategic architecture* will continue to evolve.

- The text is seminal since the concepts are constant—only the terminology changes.

Potential

Though C. K. Prahalad and Gary Hamel's "The Core Competence of the Corporation" was originally published in 1990, it is still relevant today.

Google—a company that did not exist at the time the article was first published—is a very good example of a corporation that understands the power of identifying competencies and arranging everything to support them. They have incorporated the ideas of core competencies and strategic architecture into their corporate strategy.

Changing times and circumstances, then, have not diminished the usefulness of Prahalad and Hamel's ideas. And many other examples can be found. They warn, for instance, against the idea of a company exiting a market with the intention of coming back later, using Motorola as an example. Considering that Google acquired Motorola, this is one example where they have been proven right.

Prahalad and Hamel also criticized "the tyranny of the strategic business units,"* as they called them. Organizational structures* with business units all acting independently from each other tend to result

> **❝My goal in writing this book was not to predict the future of management, but to help you invent it.❞**
>
> Gary Hamel with Bill Breen, *The Future of Management*

in corporations getting caught up with short-term goals, such as focusing on immediate sales without examining their processes and using insular—that is, idiosyncratic and somewhat narrow—practices.

In their analyses, Prahalad and Hamel found that this way of doing things, common amongst many Western companies, was one reason why they were not as successful as their Asian rivals. As many corporations today still employ this business unit organizational structure, there is potential for more development in this area.

In an increasingly globalized* world, strategic management* as a discipline will always be evolving. Researchers, business managers, and management consultants will always be searching for that competitive edge, or that idea to take corporate strategy to another level—as Prahalad and Hamel did with "The Core Competence of the Corporation."

Originally it was only capital that was highly mobile. Now other resources, including people, can be easily moved and employed elsewhere. This increases the need for companies to refine and redefine their competitive advantage. There is therefore huge potential for further development and refinement of the ideas of management strategists such as Prahalad and Hamel.

Future Directions

With the publication of "The Core Competence of the Corporation," C. K. Prahalad and Gary Hamel changed the world of strategic management—a discipline extremely broad in its effect. But this article, while falling within the domain of strategic management, has also contributed to a number of other ideas that may not necessarily be considered as obviously related to that field. Amongst these is the concept of "organizational learning."*

Strategy researchers have tended to come from disciplines such as economics, psychology, and sociology. So it is not surprising that the subject attracts divergent thinking and eclectic views on theories; Prahalad and Hamel's influence is widespread and notably diverse.

At the time of publication in 1990, there was not much concept of "outsourcing",* "re-engineering,"* and "transformation"* as essential management strategies. While no one can predict the future, it can be said with some certainty that there will be new management strategies in the future based on self-acquired organizational knowledge ("core competence") and on a plan to reach the stated goal ("strategic architecture"). One scholar who may push this area of research forward is Christopher Myers,* a professor at Harvard Business School whose work focuses on how individual learning interacts with the overall learning of organizations.

Summary

"The Core Competence of the Corporation" is one of the most reprinted papers in the history of the *Harvard Business Review*.*[1] The authors, C. K. Prahalad and Gary Hamel, are considered business gurus who had a truly significant influence on the field of strategic management and took the concept of strategy to a new level.

Taking a practical and down-to-earth approach, they illustrate to business managers how to be successful in an everyday competitive environment. While very much associated with gaining basic competitive advantages, the concept of "core competencies" has become a common term appearing in most management theories (knowledge management* and human resource management* among them). The concept of "strategic architecture" has not been as successful, having failed to replace the more entrenched idea of "strategic planning."

Prahalad and Hamel co-authored a number of strategic management texts, each building on their previous work. Each had an impact as the authors challenged the then current ideas on corporate strategy, so challenging the thinking of business managers. If the ideas were not always new, the way they were packaged and presented certainly was.

Because the ideas articulated in "The Core Competence of the Corporation" are fundamental to creating strategy, they have the potential to continue to be important. Indeed, their importance may be increasing as the strategic importance of the development of people—"human capital"—is receiving increasing recognition. People are at the heart of the concepts of core competence and strategic architecture.

NOTES

1   J. Shippmann et al., "The Practice of Competency Modeling," *Personnel Psychology* 53, no. 3 (2000): 712.

GLOSSARY

GLOSSARY OF TERMS

A. T. Kearney: a global management consulting firm who specialize in advising corporations on strategic matters.

Antitrust laws: US competition laws aimed at ensuring fair competition in a free and open market so that consumers are not exploited.

Business strategy: the theory and practice of planning business affairs with the aim of achieving specific goals such as profit, growth, or market dominance.

Cold War: a global political conflict between the predominantly capitalist countries of the United States and Western Europe and the predominantly communist countries affiliated with the Soviet Union and Eastern Europe.

Comparative advantage: the ability of an organization to produce a good or a service at a lower cost than its competitors.

Competitive advantage: the ability of an organization to outperform its competitors by offering customers better value.

Core competencies: roughly, a particular organization's collective knowledge, skills, and technologies, which together amount to that organization's unique competitive advantage.

Corporate culture: refers to the vision, norms, assumptions, and principles that members of an organization subscribe to that help define their collective identity.

Cost leadership: an economic term meaning the lowest cost of operation in the industry.

Cost-price elasticity: an economic term that measures the responsiveness of demand for a certain product or service following a change in the price of a related product or service.

Differentiation: an economic term referring to efforts by a company to make their products distinctive in the marketplace.

Diversification: the extension of business activities into disparate fields, activities, or market sectors.

Emergent strategy: the term for strategy emerging from events that have affected the pursuit of the intended strategy.

Globalization: the trend toward increasing integration in trade, technology, communications, and culture around the world.

Global strategy: the theory and practice of conducting business across international markets with the aim of meeting aims and obligations specific to the business.

Harvard Business Review: a business magazine published by Harvard Business Publishing, considered to be one of the leading publications for ideas related to business strategy, management, and leadership.

Human resource management: the management of the people who work for a business with the aim of most effectively achieving that business's goals; this usually includes things such as recruitment policy and the effective allocation of tasks to staff, and so on.

Knowledge management: the means by which organizational knowledge is obtained, pooled, developed, and employed in order to achieve specific business goals.

Korean War: a war fought between 1950 and 1953 which began as a civil war between North and South Korea but became international when the United Nations joined to support South Korea and China entered to aid North Korea.

Market segmentation: the division of a market into smaller sections such as classes of consumers, for example, or even countries, so that a business strategy can be developed to best address each section.

MBA: Master of Business Administration—a graduate degree that gives students the opportunity to develop the skills they need for careers in business management.

McKinsey Award: an award made annually by McKinsey & Company and *Harvard Business Review* recognizing the best articles published in the journal.

New games strategies: a contemporary school of thought that maintains competitive advantage is generated internally through innovation. This encompasses not only new products and services but also new ways of doing business.

Occupation of Japan: the military occupation of Japan by the United States and its allies from 1945 to 1952, during which many political, social, and economic reforms were carried out.

Organizational learning: the process by which knowledge is generated and shared across all the structures of an organization.

Organizational structure: the coordinated distribution of labor and management tasks designed to further an organization's objectives.

Outsourcing: the policy of contracting out "non-core" services or production tasks to a third-party business.

Padma Bhushan: India's third highest civil award, granted for distinguished service to the Indian nation.

Portfolio: the collection of the products, services, and achievements of the company that creates its presence in the market.

Re-engineering: the process of restructuring an organization's internal practices (workflows and management hierarchies, for example) with the intention of achieving aims such as increased efficiency, increased innovation, increased organizational learning, and so on.

Resource-based view: an approach that emphasizes a company's internal potential, rather than looking outwards to fluctuating trends in the marketplace.

Soviet Union: a communist state that existed from 1922 to 1991 that incorporated several countries of what is today Eastern Europe and Russia.

Strategic architecture: a framework useful for the achievement of a competitive advantage identifying which competencies ought to be developed and determining the technology, staffing, and other resources required to support these competencies.

Strategic business units: autonomous divisions or organizational units, each responsible for their own products and profitability.

Strategic management: the conducting of business affairs with the aim of meeting specific aims or targets unique to the business in question.

Strategy: the theory and practice of planning business affairs with the aim of achieving specific goals such as profit, growth, or market dominance.

SWOT: refers to the strategy analysis of strengths, weaknesses, opportunities, and threats.

Transformation: the process of altering a business in fundamental ways to address changes in the market.

World Resources Institute: a non-governmental organization founded with the aim of promoting the achievement of prosperity and wealth equality through the management of sustainable natural resources.

World War II (1939–45): the most widespread military conflict in history, resulting in more than 50 million casualties. While the conflict began with Germany's invasion of Poland in 1939, it soon involved all of the major world powers formed into two military alliances.

***Zaibatsu*:** a Japanese term referring to large, usually family-owned business enterprises in Japan that dominated parts of its economy before World War II.

PEOPLE MENTIONED IN THE TEXT

Kenneth R. Andrews (1919–2005) was a Harvard Business School professor. He researched extensively in business policy, corporate strategy and governance, business education, and executive education.

H. Igor Ansoff (1918–2002) was a professor, mathematician, and scientist. He is known as "the father of strategic management."

Jay Barney is Presidential Professor of Strategic Management and Pierre Lassonde Chair of Social Entrepreneurship at the University of Utah. His research interests include the links between skills and capabilities, and competitive advantage, while as a business consultant he advises on strategic organizational change.

Michael Beer is Cahners-Rabb Professor of Business Administration and Emeritus Professor at the Harvard Business School. His research focuses on organization effectiveness, organizational change, high performance organizations, leadership, and human resource management.

Alfred D. Chandler (1918–2007) was a business historian who was highly influential in business history, management, and organizational studies. He is credited with shaping the way the modern corporation is viewed.

Yves Doz is a professor of strategic management at the international graduate business school INSEAD. His research focuses on the strategy and organization of multinational corporations.

Peter Drucker (1909–2005) was a business scholar and consultant; he is sometimes referred to as "the man who invented management."

His work was highly influential on the development of modern management styles in commercial organizations.

Thomas Durand is a professor at École Centrale Paris, specializing in strategic competitive analysis and organizational change.

Bill Gates (b. 1955) founded the software company Microsoft in 1975. He is a philanthropist, inventor, computer programmer, and author.

Bruce Henderson (1915–92) was a management consultant and scholar who founded the Boston Consulting Group, one of the leading management consulting firms, in 1963.

Robert Kaplan (b. 1940) is the Marvin Bower Professor of Leadership Development, Emeritus at Harvard Business School. His research interests focus on the relationship of cost and performance management systems with strategy implementation.

Daniel Levinthal is professor of corporate strategy at the Wharton School of the University of Pennsylvania.

John Micklethwait (b. 1962) is a journalist. Former editor-in-chief of *The Economist*, he is now with Bloomberg News. His specialty is globalization and the global economy and, as editor, he expanded the international section of the magazine.

Henry Mintzberg (b. 1939) is the John Cleghorn Professor of Management Studies Strategy and Organization at McGill University, Montreal. His research interests are general management and organization, devoting his career to understanding how people actually manage.

Christopher Myers is an American professor at Harvard Business School whose work emphasizes individual learning within organizations.

David Norton (b. 1941) is a leading authority on strategic performance management and co-founder of several professional services firms.

Gary Pisano is the Harry E. Figgie Professor of Business Administration at the Harvard Business School. As a researcher, teacher, and consultant his interests include the management of innovation and intellectual property, and manufacturing and outsourcing strategy.

Michael Porter (b. 1947) is Bishop William Lawrence University Professor at Harvard Business School and the director of the school's Institute for Strategy and Competitiveness. He is considered to be a leading authority on competitive strategy.

Amy Shuen is most noted as an authority on the Silicon Valley business model and innovation economics with research interests in business strategy.

Shirish Srivastava is an associate professor at HEC School of Management, Paris. His interests cover offshore sourcing, new collaborative technologies, and technology enabled innovation.

Frederick Winslow Taylor (1856–1915) was a highly influential American inventor, engineer, and scholar. His book *The Principles of Scientific Management* was one of the first systematic studies of business management.

David Teece (b. 1948) is a professor in global business and director of the Tusher Center on Intellectual Capital at the Haas School of Business at the University of California, Berkeley. Also a business consultant, he is an expert on matters such as corporate strategy, competition policy, innovation, and entrepreneurship.

Michael Treacy is president of a boutique consulting firm. He is considered to be a leader in the consulting industry on growth strategies.

Fred Wiersema is an author and consultant specializing in strategy and market leadership. His greatest contribution has been the development of the value and growth sub-disciplines.

Adrian Wooldridge is a journalist and management writer for *The Economist*, and is now its management editor. With a major interest in globalization and business, he also writes on entrepreneurship, culture, education, and American politics.

Robert Yin (b. 1941) is a social scientist, most noted for his work on case study research.

WORKS CITED

WORKS CITED

A. T. Kearney. "The History of Strategy and Its Future Prospects." Chicago: A. T. Kearney Inc., 2014.

Andrews, Kenneth R. *The Concept of Corporate Strategy*. Homewood, IL: Richard D. Irwin, 1971.

Ansoff, H. Igor. *Corporate Strategy: An Analytical Approach to Business Policy for Growth and Expansion*. New York: McGraw-Hill, 1965.

Barber, Felix, and Rainer Strack. "The Surprising Economics of a 'People Business.'" *Harvard Business Review* 83, no. 6 (2005): 80–90.

Barney, Jay. "Firm Resources and Sustained Competitive Advantage." *Journal of Management* 17, no. 1 (1991): 99–121.

Čater, T. "Capability-Based School of Thought's Relevance and Firms' Competitive Advantage Sources." *Zagreb International Review of Economics and Business* 7, no. 1 (2004): 39–59.

Chandler, Alfred. *The Visible Hand: The Managerial Revolution in American Business*. Cambridge, MA: Harvard University Press, 1977.

Charan, Ram, and R. Edward Freeman. "Planning for the Business Environment of the 1980s." *Journal of Business Strategy* 1, no. 2 (1980): 9–19.

Crossan, Mary, and Iris Bedrow. "Organizational Learning and Strategic Renewal." *Strategic Management Journal* 24, no. 11 (2003): 1087–105.

Crossan, Mary, Henry Lane, and Roderick White. "An Organizational Learning Framework: from Intuition to Institution." *Academic Management Review* 24, no. 3 (1999): 522–37.

Drucker, Peter F. *Managing for Results: Economic Tasks and Risk-Taking Decisions*. London: Heinemann, 1964.

Durand, Thomas. "Strategizing Innovation: Competence Analysis in Assessing Strategic Change." In *Competence-Based Strategic Management*, edited by Aimé Heene and Ron Sanchez, 127–50. New York: John Wiley & Sons, 1997.

"The Alchemy of Competence." In *Strategic Flexibility: Managing in a Turbulent Environment*, edited by Gary Hamel, C. K. Prahalad, Howard Thomas, and Donald E. O'Neal, 303–30. London: John Wiley & Sons, 1998.

The Economist. "Core Competence." September 15, 2008.

Finger, M., and S. B. Brand, *The Concept of the "Learning Organization" Applied to the Transformation of the Public Sector*. Thousand Oaks, CA: Sage, 1999.

Foss, Nicolai J. "Wither the Competitive Perspective?" In *Towards a Competence Theory of the Firm,* edited by Nicolai J. Foss and Christian Knudsen, 175–200. London: Routledge, 1996.

Hamel, Gary. "Gary Hamel." Accessed March 20, 2015. http://www.garyhamel.com/.

Hamel, Gary, with Bill Breen. *The Future of Management*. Boston, MA: Harvard Business School Press, 2007.

Hamel, Gary, and C. K. Prahalad. "Strategic Intent." *Harvard Business Review* 67, no. 3 (1989): 63–76.

"Strategy as Stretch and Leverage." *Harvard Business Review* 71, no. 2 (1993): 75–84.

Competing for the Future. Boston, MA: Harvard Business Review Press, 1996.

Harvard Business Review. *HBR's 10 Must Reads: The Essentials*. Boston, MA: Harvard Business Review, 2010.

Huff, Anne S., and Rhonda K. Reger. "A Review of Strategic Process Research." *Journal of Management* 13, no. 2 (1987): 211–36.

Jabłoński, M. "The Methodology of Analyzing the Organization's Intellectual Capital." *Argumenta Oeconomica* 23, no. 2 (2009): 97–112.

Kaplan, Robert S., and David P. Norton. *The Balanced Scorecard: Translating Strategy into Action*. Boston, MA: Harvard Business Review Press, 1996.

Kay, John. *Foundations of Corporate Success: How Business Strategies Add Value*. Oxford: Oxford University Press, 1995.

Kiernan, Matthew J. "The New Strategic Architecture: Learning to Compete in the Twenty-First Century." *Academy of Management Perspectives* 7, no. 1 (1993): 7–21.

Kogut, Bruce, and Udo Zander. "Knowledge of the Firm, Combinative Capabilities, and the Replication of Technology." *Organization Science* 3, no. 3 (1992): 383–97.

Kruse, K. "What is Leadership?" *Forbes*, April 9, 2013. Accessed March 20, 2015. http://www.forbes.com/sites/kevinkruse/2013/04/09/what-is-leadership/.

Legge, K. *Power, Innovation and Problem Solving in Personnel Management*. Maidenhead: McGraw-Hill, 1978.

Lehesvirta, Tuija. "Learning Processes in a Work Organization: From Individual to Collective and/or Vice Versa?" *Journal of Workplace Learning* 16, no. 1/2 (2004): 92–100.

Levinthal, Daniel, and Jennifer Myatt. "Co-Evolution of Capabilities and Industry: The Evolution of Mutual Fund Processing." *Strategic Management Journal* 15 (1994): 45–62.

Lim, J. H., T. C. Stratopoulos, and T. S. Wirjanto. "Role of IT Executives in the Firm's Ability to Achieve Competitive Advantage through IT Capability." *International Journal of Accounting Information Systems* 13, no. 1 (2012): 21–40.

Linder, Jane C., Martin I. Cole, and Alvin J. Jacobson. "Business Transformation through Outsourcing." *Strategy & Leadership* 30, no. 4 (2002): 23–28.

The Marketing People. "Apple Maps Vs. Google Maps and the Importance of Core Competencies in Strategy." September 21, 2012. Accessed March 20, 2015. http://www.themarketingpeople.com/blog/index.php/apple-maps-vs-google-maps-core-competencies-in-strategy/.

McKiernan, Peter. "Strategy Past; Strategy Futures." *Long Range Planning* 30, no. 5 (1997): 790–8.

McKinsey & Company. "The Lean Management Enterprise" (2014). http://www.mckinsey.com/client_service/operations/latest_thinking/lean_management.

Micklethwait, John, and Adrian Wooldridge. *The Witch Doctors: Making Sense of the Management Gurus*. New York: Times Books, 1996.

Mintzberg, Henry, and James A. Waters, "Of Strategies, Deliberate and Emergent." *Strategic Management Journal* 6, no. 3 (1985): 257–72.

Moore, Karl, and Phil Lenir. "Mintzberg's Better Way to Do Corporate Strategy." *Forbes*, June 21, 2011.

Namaki, M. S. S. El. "Are We Seeing a Shift in Corporate Strategy Behaviour Today?" *Ivey Business Journal* September/October (2012): 1–4.

Nobre, F. S., D. Walker, and R. J. Harris. *Technological, Managerial and Organizational Core Competencies: Dynamic Innovation and Sustainable Development*. Hershey, PA: IGI Global, 2012.

Porter, Michael E. *Interbrand Choice, Strategy and Bilateral Market Power*. Cambridge, MA: Harvard University Press, 1976.

Competitive Strategy: Techniques for Analyzing Industries and Competitors. New York: Free Press, 1980.

Competitive Advantage: Creating and Sustaining Superior Performance. New York: Free Press, 1985.

"What is Strategy?" *Harvard Business Review* 74, no. 6 (1996): 7–31.

Prahalad, C. K. "The Role of Core Competencies in the Corporation." *Research Technology Management* 36, no. 6 (1993): 40–7.

The Fortune at the Bottom of the Pyramid. Upper Saddle River, NJ: Prentice Hall, 2005.

Prahalad, C. K., and Gary Hamel. "The Core Competence of the Corporation." *Harvard Business Review* 68, no. 3 (1990): 79–91.

"Strategy as a Field of Study: Why Search for a New Paradigm?" *Strategic Management Journal* Special Issue 15 (1994): 5–16.

Prahalad, C. K., and Krishnan, M. S. *The New Age of Innovation: Driving Co-Created Value Through Global Networks*. New York: McGraw Hill, 2008.

Rasmus, Daniel W. "How Clinging to Core Competencies Is Breaking Your Organization's Heart." *Fast Company*, August 22, 2012.

Rowland, K. M., and S. L. Summers, "Human Resource Planning: A Second Look." *Personnel Administration* 26, no. 12 (1981): 73–80.

Shippmann, Jeffery S., Ronald A. Ash, Mariangela Batjtsta, Linda Carr, Lorraine D. Eyde, Beryl Hesketh, Jerry Kehoe, Kenneth Pearlman, Erich P. Prien, and Juan I. Sanchez. "The Practice of Competency Modeling." *Personnel Psychology* 53, no. 3 (2000): 703–39.

Smith, Wendell. "Product Differentiation and Market Segmentation as Alternative Marketing Strategies." *Journal of Marketing* 21, no. 1 (1956): 3–8.

Takemae, Eiji. *Inside GCHQ: The Allied Occupation of Japan and Its Legacy*. Translated by Robert Ricketts and Sebastian Swann. New York: Continuum, 2002.

Taylor, Frederick Winslow. *The Principles of Scientific Management*. New York: Harper & Brothers, 1911.

Teece, David J. "Explicating Dynamic Capabilities: The Nature and Foundations of (Sustainable) Enterprise Performance." *Strategic Management Journal* 28, no. 13 (2007): 1319–50.

Teece, David J., Gary Pisano, and Amy Shuen. "Dynamic Capabilities and Strategic Management." *Strategic Management Journal* 18, no. 17 (1997): 509–33.

Treacy, Michael, and Fred Wiersema. *The Discipline of Market Leaders: Choose Your Customers, Narrow Your Focus, Dominate Your Market*. Reading, MA: Addison-Wesley, 1995.

Wooldridge, Adrian. "The Guru at the Bottom of the Pyramid." *The Economist*, April 22, 2010.

Yin, Robert K. *Case Study Research: Designs and Methods*. Thousand Oaks, CA: Sage, 1984.

Young, Ruth. "Interview with Gary Hamel." *Strategic Direction* 25, no. 4 (2002): 30–1.

THE MACAT LIBRARY
BY DISCIPLINE

AFRICANA STUDIES

Chinua Achebe's *An Image of Africa: Racism in Conrad's Heart of Darkness*
W. E. B. Du Bois's *The Souls of Black Folk*
Zora Neale Huston's *Characteristics of Negro Expression*
Martin Luther King Jr's *Why We Can't Wait*
Toni Morrison's *Playing in the Dark: Whiteness in the American Literary Imagination*

ANTHROPOLOGY

Arjun Appadurai's *Modernity at Large: Cultural Dimensions of Globalisation*
Philippe Ariès's *Centuries of Childhood*
Franz Boas's *Race, Language and Culture*
Kim Chan & Renée Mauborgne's *Blue Ocean Strategy*
Jared Diamond's *Guns, Germs & Steel: the Fate of Human Societies*
Jared Diamond's *Collapse: How Societies Choose to Fail or Survive*
E. E. Evans-Pritchard's *Witchcraft, Oracles and Magic Among the Azande*
James Ferguson's *The Anti-Politics Machine*
Clifford Geertz's *The Interpretation of Cultures*
David Graeber's *Debt: the First 5000 Years*
Karen Ho's *Liquidated: An Ethnography of Wall Street*
Geert Hofstede's *Culture's Consequences: Comparing Values, Behaviors, Institutes and Organizations across Nations*
Claude Lévi-Strauss's *Structural Anthropology*
Jay Macleod's *Ain't No Makin' It: Aspirations and Attainment in a Low-Income Neighborhood*
Saba Mahmood's *The Politics of Piety: The Islamic Revival and the Feminist Subject*
Marcel Mauss's *The Gift*

BUSINESS

Jean Lave & Etienne Wenger's *Situated Learning*
Theodore Levitt's *Marketing Myopia*
Burton G. Malkiel's *A Random Walk Down Wall Street*
Douglas McGregor's *The Human Side of Enterprise*
Michael Porter's *Competitive Strategy: Creating and Sustaining Superior Performance*
John Kotter's *Leading Change*
C. K. Prahalad & Gary Hamel's *The Core Competence of the Corporation*

CRIMINOLOGY

Michelle Alexander's *The New Jim Crow: Mass Incarceration in the Age of Colorblindness*
Michael R. Gottfredson & Travis Hirschi's *A General Theory of Crime*
Richard Herrnstein & Charles A. Murray's *The Bell Curve: Intelligence and Class Structure in American Life*
Elizabeth Loftus's *Eyewitness Testimony*
Jay Macleod's *Ain't No Makin' It: Aspirations and Attainment in a Low-Income Neighborhood*
Philip Zimbardo's *The Lucifer Effect*

ECONOMICS

Janet Abu-Lughod's *Before European Hegemony*
Ha-Joon Chang's *Kicking Away the Ladder*
David Brion Davis's *The Problem of Slavery in the Age of Revolution*
Milton Friedman's *The Role of Monetary Policy*
Milton Friedman's *Capitalism and Freedom*
David Graeber's *Debt: the First 5000 Years*
Friedrich Hayek's *The Road to Serfdom*
Karen Ho's *Liquidated: An Ethnography of Wall Street*

The Macat Library By Discipline

John Maynard Keynes's *The General Theory of Employment, Interest and Money*
Charles P. Kindleberger's *Manias, Panics and Crashes*
Robert Lucas's *Why Doesn't Capital Flow from Rich to Poor Countries?*
Burton G. Malkiel's *A Random Walk Down Wall Street*
Thomas Robert Malthus's *An Essay on the Principle of Population*
Karl Marx's *Capital*
Thomas Piketty's *Capital in the Twenty-First Century*
Amartya Sen's *Development as Freedom*
Adam Smith's *The Wealth of Nations*
Nassim Nicholas Taleb's *The Black Swan: The Impact of the Highly Improbable*
Amos Tversky's & Daniel Kahneman's *Judgment under Uncertainty: Heuristics and Biases*
Mahbub Ul Haq's *Reflections on Human Development*
Max Weber's *The Protestant Ethic and the Spirit of Capitalism*

FEMINISM AND GENDER STUDIES

Judith Butler's *Gender Trouble*
Simone De Beauvoir's *The Second Sex*
Michel Foucault's *History of Sexuality*
Betty Friedan's *The Feminine Mystique*
Saba Mahmood's *The Politics of Piety: The Islamic Revival and the Feminist Subject*
Joan Wallach Scott's *Gender and the Politics of History*
Mary Wollstonecraft's *A Vindication of the Rights of Woman*
Virginia Woolf's *A Room of One's Own*

GEOGRAPHY

The Brundtland Report's *Our Common Future*
Rachel Carson's *Silent Spring*
Charles Darwin's *On the Origin of Species*
James Ferguson's *The Anti-Politics Machine*
Jane Jacobs's *The Death and Life of Great American Cities*
James Lovelock's *Gaia: A New Look at Life on Earth*
Amartya Sen's *Development as Freedom*
Mathis Wackernagel & William Rees's *Our Ecological Footprint*

HISTORY

Janet Abu-Lughod's *Before European Hegemony*
Benedict Anderson's *Imagined Communities*
Bernard Bailyn's *The Ideological Origins of the American Revolution*
Hanna Batatu's *The Old Social Classes And The Revolutionary Movements Of Iraq*
Christopher Browning's *Ordinary Men: Reserve Police Batallion 101 and the Final Solution in Poland*
Edmund Burke's *Reflections on the Revolution in France*
William Cronon's *Nature's Metropolis: Chicago And The Great West*
Alfred W. Crosby's *The Columbian Exchange*
Hamid Dabashi's *Iran: A People Interrupted*
David Brion Davis's *The Problem of Slavery in the Age of Revolution*
Nathalie Zemon Davis's *The Return of Martin Guerre*
Jared Diamond's *Guns, Germs & Steel: the Fate of Human Societies*
Frank Dikotter's *Mao's Great Famine*
John W Dower's *War Without Mercy: Race And Power In The Pacific War*
W. E. B. Du Bois's *The Souls of Black Folk*
Richard J. Evans's *In Defence of History*
Lucien Febvre's *The Problem of Unbelief in the 16th Century*
Sheila Fitzpatrick's *Everyday Stalinism*

Eric Foner's *Reconstruction: America's Unfinished Revolution, 1863-1877*
Michel Foucault's *Discipline and Punish*
Michel Foucault's *History of Sexuality*
Francis Fukuyama's *The End of History and the Last Man*
John Lewis Gaddis's *We Now Know: Rethinking Cold War History*
Ernest Gellner's *Nations and Nationalism*
Eugene Genovese's *Roll, Jordan, Roll: The World the Slaves Made*
Carlo Ginzburg's *The Night Battles*
Daniel Goldhagen's *Hitler's Willing Executioners*
Jack Goldstone's *Revolution and Rebellion in the Early Modern World*
Antonio Gramsci's *The Prison Notebooks*
Alexander Hamilton, John Jay & James Madison's *The Federalist Papers*
Christopher Hill's *The World Turned Upside Down*
Carole Hillenbrand's *The Crusades: Islamic Perspectives*
Thomas Hobbes's *Leviathan*
Eric Hobsbawm's *The Age Of Revolution*
John A. Hobson's *Imperialism: A Study*
Albert Hourani's *History of the Arab Peoples*
Samuel P. Huntington's *The Clash of Civilizations and the Remaking of World Order*
C. L. R. James's *The Black Jacobins*
Tony Judt's *Postwar: A History of Europe Since 1945*
Ernst Kantorowicz's *The King's Two Bodies: A Study in Medieval Political Theology*
Paul Kennedy's *The Rise and Fall of the Great Powers*
Ian Kershaw's *The "Hitler Myth": Image and Reality in the Third Reich*
John Maynard Keynes's *The General Theory of Employment, Interest and Money*
Charles P. Kindleberger's *Manias, Panics and Crashes*
Martin Luther King Jr's *Why We Can't Wait*
Henry Kissinger's *World Order: Reflections on the Character of Nations and the Course of History*
Thomas Kuhn's *The Structure of Scientific Revolutions*
Georges Lefebvre's *The Coming of the French Revolution*
John Locke's *Two Treatises of Government*
Niccolò Machiavelli's *The Prince*
Thomas Robert Malthus's *An Essay on the Principle of Population*
Mahmood Mamdani's *Citizen and Subject: Contemporary Africa And The Legacy Of Late Colonialism*
Karl Marx's *Capital*
Stanley Milgram's *Obedience to Authority*
John Stuart Mill's *On Liberty*
Thomas Paine's *Common Sense*
Thomas Paine's *Rights of Man*
Geoffrey Parker's *Global Crisis: War, Climate Change and Catastrophe in the Seventeenth Century*
Jonathan Riley-Smith's *The First Crusade and the Idea of Crusading*
Jean-Jacques Rousseau's *The Social Contract*
Joan Wallach Scott's *Gender and the Politics of History*
Theda Skocpol's *States and Social Revolutions*
Adam Smith's *The Wealth of Nations*
Timothy Snyder's *Bloodlands: Europe Between Hitler and Stalin*
Sun Tzu's *The Art of War*
Keith Thomas's *Religion and the Decline of Magic*
Thucydides's *The History of the Peloponnesian War*
Frederick Jackson Turner's *The Significance of the Frontier in American History*
Odd Arne Westad's *The Global Cold War: Third World Interventions And The Making Of Our Times*

The Macat Library By Discipline

LITERATURE

Chinua Achebe's *An Image of Africa: Racism in Conrad's Heart of Darkness*
Roland Barthes's *Mythologies*
Homi K. Bhabha's *The Location of Culture*
Judith Butler's *Gender Trouble*
Simone De Beauvoir's *The Second Sex*
Ferdinand De Saussure's *Course in General Linguistics*
T. S. Eliot's *The Sacred Wood: Essays on Poetry and Criticism*
Zora Neale Huston's *Characteristics of Negro Expression*
Toni Morrison's *Playing in the Dark: Whiteness in the American Literary Imagination*
Edward Said's *Orientalism*
Gayatri Chakravorty Spivak's *Can the Subaltern Speak?*
Mary Wollstonecraft's *A Vindication of the Rights of Women*
Virginia Woolf's *A Room of One's Own*

PHILOSOPHY

Elizabeth Anscombe's *Modern Moral Philosophy*
Hannah Arendt's *The Human Condition*
Aristotle's *Metaphysics*
Aristotle's *Nicomachean Ethics*
Edmund Gettier's *Is Justified True Belief Knowledge?*
Georg Wilhelm Friedrich Hegel's *Phenomenology of Spirit*
David Hume's *Dialogues Concerning Natural Religion*
David Hume's *The Enquiry for Human Understanding*
Immanuel Kant's *Religion within the Boundaries of Mere Reason*
Immanuel Kant's *Critique of Pure Reason*
Søren Kierkegaard's *The Sickness Unto Death*
Søren Kierkegaard's *Fear and Trembling*
C. S. Lewis's *The Abolition of Man*
Alasdair MacIntyre's *After Virtue*
Marcus Aurelius's *Meditations*
Friedrich Nietzsche's *On the Genealogy of Morality*
Friedrich Nietzsche's *Beyond Good and Evil*
Plato's *Republic*
Plato's *Symposium*
Jean-Jacques Rousseau's *The Social Contract*
Gilbert Ryle's *The Concept of Mind*
Baruch Spinoza's *Ethics*
Sun Tzu's *The Art of War*
Ludwig Wittgenstein's *Philosophical Investigations*

POLITICS

Benedict Anderson's *Imagined Communities*
Aristotle's *Politics*
Bernard Bailyn's *The Ideological Origins of the American Revolution*
Edmund Burke's *Reflections on the Revolution in France*
John C. Calhoun's *A Disquisition on Government*
Ha-Joon Chang's *Kicking Away the Ladder*
Hamid Dabashi's *Iran: A People Interrupted*
Hamid Dabashi's *Theology of Discontent: The Ideological Foundation of the Islamic Revolution in Iran*
Robert Dahl's *Democracy and its Critics*
Robert Dahl's *Who Governs?*
David Brion Davis's *The Problem of Slavery in the Age of Revolution*

Alexis De Tocqueville's *Democracy in America*
James Ferguson's *The Anti-Politics Machine*
Frank Dikotter's *Mao's Great Famine*
Sheila Fitzpatrick's *Everyday Stalinism*
Eric Foner's *Reconstruction: America's Unfinished Revolution, 1863-1877*
Milton Friedman's *Capitalism and Freedom*
Francis Fukuyama's *The End of History and the Last Man*
John Lewis Gaddis's *We Now Know: Rethinking Cold War History*
Ernest Gellner's *Nations and Nationalism*
David Graeber's *Debt: the First 5000 Years*
Antonio Gramsci's *The Prison Notebooks*
Alexander Hamilton, John Jay & James Madison's *The Federalist Papers*
Friedrich Hayek's *The Road to Serfdom*
Christopher Hill's *The World Turned Upside Down*
Thomas Hobbes's *Leviathan*
John A. Hobson's *Imperialism: A Study*
Samuel P. Huntington's *The Clash of Civilizations and the Remaking of World Order*
Tony Judt's *Postwar: A History of Europe Since 1945*
David C. Kang's *China Rising: Peace, Power and Order in East Asia*
Paul Kennedy's *The Rise and Fall of Great Powers*
Robert Keohane's *After Hegemony*
Martin Luther King Jr.'s *Why We Can't Wait*
Henry Kissinger's *World Order: Reflections on the Character of Nations and the Course of History*
John Locke's *Two Treatises of Government*
Niccolò Machiavelli's *The Prince*
Thomas Robert Malthus's *An Essay on the Principle of Population*
Mahmood Mamdani's *Citizen and Subject: Contemporary Africa And The Legacy Of Late Colonialism*
Karl Marx's *Capital*
John Stuart Mill's *On Liberty*
John Stuart Mill's *Utilitarianism*
Hans Morgenthau's *Politics Among Nations*
Thomas Paine's *Common Sense*
Thomas Paine's *Rights of Man*
Thomas Piketty's *Capital in the Twenty-First Century*
Robert D. Putman's *Bowling Alone*
John Rawls's *Theory of Justice*
Jean-Jacques Rousseau's *The Social Contract*
Theda Skocpol's *States and Social Revolutions*
Adam Smith's *The Wealth of Nations*
Sun Tzu's *The Art of War*
Henry David Thoreau's *Civil Disobedience*
Thucydides's *The History of the Peloponnesian War*
Kenneth Waltz's *Theory of International Politics*
Max Weber's *Politics as a Vocation*
Odd Arne Westad's *The Global Cold War: Third World Interventions And The Making Of Our Times*

POSTCOLONIAL STUDIES

Roland Barthes's *Mythologies*
Frantz Fanon's *Black Skin, White Masks*
Homi K. Bhabha's *The Location of Culture*
Gustavo Gutiérrez's *A Theology of Liberation*
Edward Said's *Orientalism*
Gayatri Chakravorty Spivak's *Can the Subaltern Speak?*

The Macat Library By Discipline

PSYCHOLOGY

Gordon Allport's *The Nature of Prejudice*
Alan Baddeley & Graham Hitch's *Aggression: A Social Learning Analysis*
Albert Bandura's *Aggression: A Social Learning Analysis*
Leon Festinger's *A Theory of Cognitive Dissonance*
Sigmund Freud's *The Interpretation of Dreams*
Betty Friedan's *The Feminine Mystique*
Michael R. Gottfredson & Travis Hirschi's *A General Theory of Crime*
Eric Hoffer's *The True Believer: Thoughts on the Nature of Mass Movements*
William James's *Principles of Psychology*
Elizabeth Loftus's *Eyewitness Testimony*
A. H. Maslow's *A Theory of Human Motivation*
Stanley Milgram's *Obedience to Authority*
Steven Pinker's *The Better Angels of Our Nature*
Oliver Sacks's *The Man Who Mistook His Wife For a Hat*
Richard Thaler & Cass Sunstein's *Nudge: Improving Decisions About Health, Wealth and Happiness*
Amos Tversky's *Judgment under Uncertainty: Heuristics and Biases*
Philip Zimbardo's *The Lucifer Effect*

SCIENCE

Rachel Carson's *Silent Spring*
William Cronon's *Nature's Metropolis: Chicago And The Great West*
Alfred W. Crosby's *The Columbian Exchange*
Charles Darwin's *On the Origin of Species*
Richard Dawkin's *The Selfish Gene*
Thomas Kuhn's *The Structure of Scientific Revolutions*
Geoffrey Parker's *Global Crisis: War, Climate Change and Catastrophe in the Seventeenth Century*
Mathis Wackernagel & William Rees's *Our Ecological Footprint*

SOCIOLOGY

Michelle Alexander's *The New Jim Crow: Mass Incarceration in the Age of Colorblindness*
Gordon Allport's *The Nature of Prejudice*
Albert Bandura's *Aggression: A Social Learning Analysis*
Hanna Batatu's *The Old Social Classes And The Revolutionary Movements Of Iraq*
Ha-Joon Chang's *Kicking Away the Ladder*
W. E. B. Du Bois's *The Souls of Black Folk*
Émile Durkheim's *On Suicide*
Frantz Fanon's *Black Skin, White Masks*
Frantz Fanon's *The Wretched of the Earth*
Eric Foner's *Reconstruction: America's Unfinished Revolution, 1863-1877*
Eugene Genovese's *Roll, Jordan, Roll: The World the Slaves Made*
Jack Goldstone's *Revolution and Rebellion in the Early Modern World*
Antonio Gramsci's *The Prison Notebooks*
Richard Herrnstein & Charles A Murray's *The Bell Curve: Intelligence and Class Structure in American Life*
Eric Hoffer's *The True Believer: Thoughts on the Nature of Mass Movements*
Jane Jacobs's *The Death and Life of Great American Cities*
Robert Lucas's *Why Doesn't Capital Flow from Rich to Poor Countries?*
Jay Macleod's *Ain't No Makin' It: Aspirations and Attainment in a Low Income Neighborhood*
Elaine May's *Homeward Bound: American Families in the Cold War Era*
Douglas McGregor's *The Human Side of Enterprise*
C. Wright Mills's *The Sociological Imagination*

Thomas Piketty's *Capital in the Twenty-First Century*
Robert D. Putman's *Bowling Alone*
David Riesman's *The Lonely Crowd: A Study of the Changing American Character*
Edward Said's *Orientalism*
Joan Wallach Scott's *Gender and the Politics of History*
Theda Skocpol's *States and Social Revolutions*
Max Weber's *The Protestant Ethic and the Spirit of Capitalism*

THEOLOGY

Augustine's *Confessions*
Benedict's *Rule of St Benedict*
Gustavo Gutiérrez's *A Theology of Liberation*
Carole Hillenbrand's *The Crusades: Islamic Perspectives*
David Hume's *Dialogues Concerning Natural Religion*
Immanuel Kant's *Religion within the Boundaries of Mere Reason*
Ernst Kantorowicz's *The King's Two Bodies: A Study in Medieval Political Theology*
Søren Kierkegaard's *The Sickness Unto Death*
C. S. Lewis's *The Abolition of Man*
Saba Mahmood's *The Politics of Piety: The Islamic Revival and the Feminist Subject*
Baruch Spinoza's *Ethics*
Keith Thomas's *Religion and the Decline of Magic*

COMING SOON

Chris Argyris's *The Individual and the Organisation*
Seyla Benhabib's *The Rights of Others*
Walter Benjamin's *The Work Of Art in the Age of Mechanical Reproduction*
John Berger's *Ways of Seeing*
Pierre Bourdieu's *Outline of a Theory of Practice*
Mary Douglas's *Purity and Danger*
Roland Dworkin's *Taking Rights Seriously*
James G. March's *Exploration and Exploitation in Organisational Learning*
Ikujiro Nonaka's *A Dynamic Theory of Organizational Knowledge Creation*
Griselda Pollock's *Vision and Difference*
Amartya Sen's *Inequality Re-Examined*
Susan Sontag's *On Photography*
Yasser Tabbaa's *The Transformation of Islamic Art*
Ludwig von Mises's *Theory of Money and Credit*

Macat Disciplines

Access the greatest ideas and thinkers across entire disciplines, including

AFRICANA STUDIES

Chinua Achebe's *An Image of Africa: Racism in Conrad's Heart of Darkness*

W. E. B. Du Bois's *The Souls of Black Folk*

Zora Neale Hurston's *Characteristics of Negro Expression*

Martin Luther King Jr.'s *Why We Can't Wait*

Toni Morrison's *Playing in the Dark: Whiteness in the American Literary Imagination*

Macat analyses are available from all good bookshops and libraries.

Access hundreds of analyses through one, multimedia tool.
Join free for one month **library.macat.com**

Macat Disciplines

Access the greatest ideas and thinkers across entire disciplines, including

MACAT

FEMINISM, GENDER AND QUEER STUDIES

Simone De Beauvoir's
The Second Sex

Michel Foucault's
History of Sexuality

Betty Friedan's
The Feminine Mystique

Saba Mahmood's
*The Politics of Piety:
The Islamic Revival and
the Feminist Subject*

Joan Wallach Scott's
*Gender and the
Politics of History*

Mary Wollstonecraft's
*A Vindication of the
Rights of Woman*

Virginia Woolf's
A Room of One's Own

Judith Butler's
Gender Trouble

Macat analyses are available from all good bookshops and libraries.

Access hundreds of analyses through one, multimedia tool.

Join free for one month **library.macat.com**

Macat Disciplines

Access the greatest ideas and thinkers across entire disciplines, including

CRIMINOLOGY

Michelle Alexander's
The New Jim Crow: Mass Incarceration in the Age of Colorblindness

Michael R. Gottfredson & Travis Hirschi's
A General Theory of Crime

Elizabeth Loftus's
Eyewitness Testimony

Richard Herrnstein & Charles A. Murray's
The Bell Curve: Intelligence and Class Structure in American Life

Jay Macleod's
Ain't No Makin' It: Aspirations and Attainment in a Low-Income Neighborhood

Philip Zimbardo's
The Lucifer Effect

Macat analyses are available from all good bookshops and libraries.

Access hundreds of analyses through one, multimedia tool.
Join free for one month **library.macat.com**

Macat Disciplines

Access the greatest ideas and thinkers across entire disciplines, including

INEQUALITY

Ha-Joon Chang's, *Kicking Away the Ladder*

David Graeber's, *Debt: The First 5000 Years*

Robert E. Lucas's, *Why Doesn't Capital Flow from Rich To Poor Countries?*

Thomas Piketty's, *Capital in the Twenty-First Century*

Amartya Sen's, *Inequality Re-Examined*

Mahbub Ul Haq's, *Reflections on Human Development*

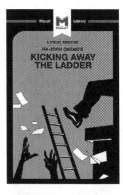  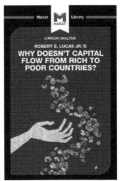

Macat analyses are available from all good bookshops and libraries.

Access hundreds of analyses through one, multimedia tool.
Join free for one month **library.macat.com**

Macat Disciplines

*Access the greatest ideas and thinkers
across entire disciplines, including*

GLOBALIZATION

Arjun Appadurai's, *Modernity at Large:
Cultural Dimensions of Globalisation*

James Ferguson's, *The Anti-Politics Machine*

Geert Hofstede's, *Culture's Consequences*

Amartya Sen's, *Development as Freedom*

Macat Disciplines

Access the greatest ideas and thinkers across entire disciplines, including

MAN AND THE ENVIRONMENT

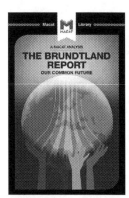

The Brundtland Report's, *Our Common Future*
Rachel Carson's, *Silent Spring*
James Lovelock's, *Gaia: A New Look at Life on Earth*
Mathis Wackernagel & William Rees's, *Our Ecological Footprint*

Macat analyses are available from all good bookshops and libraries.

Access hundreds of analyses through one, multimedia tool.
Join free for one month **library.macat.com**

Macat Disciplines

*Access the greatest ideas and thinkers
across entire disciplines, including*

THE FUTURE OF DEMOCRACY

Robert A. Dahl's, *Democracy and Its Critics*
Robert A. Dahl's, *Who Governs?*
Alexis De Toqueville's, *Democracy in America*
Niccolò Machiavelli's, *The Prince*
John Stuart Mill's, *On Liberty*
Robert D. Putnam's, *Bowling Alone*
Jean-Jacques Rousseau's, *The Social Contract*
Henry David Thoreau's, *Civil Disobedience*

Macat Disciplines

Access the greatest ideas and thinkers across entire disciplines, including

MACAT

TOTALITARIANISM

Sheila Fitzpatrick's, *Everyday Stalinism*
Ian Kershaw's, *The "Hitler Myth"*
Timothy Snyder's, *Bloodlands*

Macat analyses are available from all good bookshops and libraries.

Access hundreds of analyses through one, multimedia tool.
Join free for one month **library.macat.com**

Macat Pairs

Analyse historical and modern issues from opposite sides of an argument. Pairs include:

RACE AND IDENTITY

Zora Neale Hurston's
Characteristics of Negro Expression

Using material collected on anthropological expeditions to the South, Zora Neale Hurston explains how expression in African American culture in the early twentieth century departs from the art of white America. At the time, African American art was often criticized for copying white culture. For Hurston, this criticism misunderstood how art works. European tradition views art as something fixed. But Hurston describes a creative process that is alive, ever-changing, and largely improvisational. She maintains that African American art works through a process called 'mimicry'—where an imitated object or verbal pattern, for example, is reshaped and altered until it becomes something new, novel—and worthy of attention.

Frantz Fanon's
Black Skin, White Masks

Black Skin, White Masks offers a radical analysis of the psychological effects of colonization on the colonized.

Fanon witnessed the effects of colonization first hand both in his birthplace, Martinique, and again later in life when he worked as a psychiatrist in another French colony, Algeria. His text is uncompromising in form and argument. He dissects the dehumanizing effects of colonialism, arguing that it destroys the native sense of identity, forcing people to adapt to an alien set of values—including a core belief that they are inferior. This results in deep psychological trauma.

Fanon's work played a pivotal role in the civil rights movements of the 1960s.

Macat analyses are available from all good bookshops and libraries.

Access hundreds of analyses through one, multimedia tool.
Join free for one month **library.macat.com**

Macat Pairs

Analyse historical and modern issues from opposite sides of an argument. Pairs include:

INTERNATIONAL RELATIONS IN THE 21ˢᵀ CENTURY

Samuel P. Huntington's
The Clash of Civilisations

In his highly influential 1996 book, Huntington offers a vision of a post-Cold War world in which conflict takes place not between competing ideologies but between cultures. The worst clash, he argues, will be between the Islamic world and the West: the West's arrogance and belief that its culture is a "gift" to the world will come into conflict with Islam's obstinacy and concern that its culture is under attack from a morally decadent "other."

Clash inspired much debate between different political schools of thought. But its greatest impact came in helping define American foreign policy in the wake of the 2001 terrorist attacks in New York and Washington.

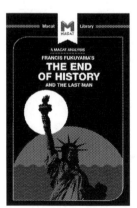

Francis Fukuyama's
The End of History and the Last Man

Published in 1992, *The End of History and the Last Man* argues that capitalist democracy is the final destination for all societies. Fukuyama believed democracy triumphed during the Cold War because it lacks the "fundamental contradictions" inherent in communism and satisfies our yearning for freedom and equality. Democracy therefore marks the endpoint in the evolution of ideology, and so the "end of history." There will still be "events," but no fundamental change in ideology.

Macat Pairs

Analyse historical and modern issues from opposite sides of an argument. Pairs include:

HOW TO RUN AN ECONOMY

John Maynard Keynes's
The General Theory OF Employment, Interest and Money

Classical economics suggests that market economies are self-correcting in times of recession or depression, and tend toward full employment and output. But English economist John Maynard Keynes disagrees.

In his ground-breaking 1936 study *The General Theory*, Keynes argues that traditional economics has misunderstood the causes of unemployment. Employment is not determined by the price of labor; it is directly linked to demand. Keynes believes market economies are by nature unstable, and so require government intervention. Spurred on by the social catastrophe of the Great Depression of the 1930s, he sets out to revolutionize the way the world thinks

Milton Friedman's
The Role of Monetary Policy

Friedman's 1968 paper changed the course of economic theory. In just 17 pages, he demolished existing theory and outlined an effective alternate monetary policy designed to secure 'high employment, stable prices and rapid growth.'

Friedman demonstrated that monetary policy plays a vital role in broader economic stability and argued that economists got their monetary policy wrong in the 1950s and 1960s by misunderstanding the relationship between inflation and unemployment. Previous generations of economists had believed that governments could permanently decrease unemployment by permitting inflation—and vice versa. Friedman's most original contribution was to show that this supposed trade-off is an illusion that only works in the short term.

Macat analyses are available from all good bookshops and libraries.

Access hundreds of analyses through one, multimedia tool.
Join free for one month **library.macat.com**

Macat Pairs

Analyse historical and modern issues from opposite sides of an argument. Pairs include:

ARE WE FUNDAMENTALLY GOOD - OR BAD?

Steven Pinker's
The Better Angels of Our Nature

Stephen Pinker's gloriously optimistic 2011 book argues that, despite humanity's biological tendency toward violence, we are, in fact, less violent today than ever before. To prove his case, Pinker lays out pages of detailed statistical evidence. For him, much of the credit for the decline goes to the eighteenth-century Enlightenment movement, whose ideas of liberty, tolerance, and respect for the value of human life filtered down through society and affected how people thought. That psychological change led to behavioral change—and overall we became more peaceful. Critics countered that humanity could never overcome the biological urge toward violence; others argued that Pinker's statistics were flawed.

Philip Zimbardo's
The Lucifer Effect

Some psychologists believe those who commit cruelty are innately evil. Zimbardo disagrees. In *The Lucifer Effect*, he argues that sometimes good people do evil things simply because of the situations they find themselves in, citing many historical examples to illustrate his point. Zimbardo details his 1971 Stanford prison experiment, where ordinary volunteers playing guards in a mock prison rapidly became abusive. But he also describes the tortures committed by US army personnel in Iraq's Abu Ghraib prison in 2003—and how he himself testified in defence of one of those guards. committed by US army personnel in Iraq's Abu Ghraib prison in 2003—and how he himself testified in defence of one of those guards.

Macat Pairs

Analyse historical and modern issues from opposite sides of an argument. Pairs include:

HOW WE RELATE TO EACH OTHER AND SOCIETY

Jean-Jacques Rousseau's
The Social Contract

Rousseau's famous work sets out the radical concept of the 'social contract': a give-and-take relationship between individual freedom and social order.

If people are free to do as they like, governed only by their own sense of justice, they are also vulnerable to chaos and violence. To avoid this, Rousseau proposes, they should agree to give up some freedom to benefit from the protection of social and political organization. But this deal is only just if societies are led by the collective needs and desires of the people, and able to control the private interests of individuals. For Rousseau, the only legitimate form of government is rule by the people.

Robert D. Putnam's
Bowling Alone

In *Bowling Alone*, Robert Putnam argues that Americans have become disconnected from one another and from the institutions of their common life, and investigates the consequences of this change.

Looking at a range of indicators, from membership in formal organizations to the number of invitations being extended to informal dinner parties, Putnam demonstrates that Americans are interacting less and creating less "social capital" – with potentially disastrous implications for their society.

It would be difficult to overstate the impact of *Bowling Alone*, one of the most frequently cited social science publications of the last half-century.

Macat analyses are available from all good bookshops and libraries.

Access hundreds of analyses through one, multimedia tool.
Join free for one month **library.macat.com**

Printed in the United States
by Baker & Taylor Publisher Services